Piano Music Book of
Bach Classics
for Beginners

No Music Reading Required!

Damon Ferrante

Teach Yourself Famous Piano Solos & Easy Piano Sheet Music, Vivaldi, Handel, Music Theory, Chords, Scales, Exercises

Book & Streaming Video Lessons

Introduction: How the Book & Videos Work

As a piano professor and piano teacher for over twenty years, I have wanted to help beginner piano students succeed in playing famous and beautiful music by the great composers. In the past, piano books on the great composers have taken a dull and uninspiring approach. Most of the time these books just throw together pieces by composers in a random, boring, and confusing way; sometimes these books are no better than blurry photocopies.

This book and video course takes a new and innovative approach!

Piano Music Book of Bach Classics for Beginners makes learning great classical piano pieces fun, easy, interactive, and engaging. The book and streaming videos follow a step-by-step lesson format for learning some of the most famous music by Bach, as well as some of the most beloved pieces by Vivaldi, Handel, Pachelbel, and Telemann. Pieces you have always dreamt about playing on the piano for yourself and for your family and friends!

In *Piano Music Book of Bach Classics for Beginners,* each lesson builds on the previous one in a clear and easy-to-understand manner. No music reading is necessary. I walk you through how to play these wonderful pieces, starting with very easy music, at the beginning of the book, and advancing, little by little, as you master new repertoire and techniques. As you are able to play these new pieces, you will also greatly improve your abilities on the piano! Along the way, you will learn to read music, play chords and scales, learn rhythms, techniques, and music theory, as well.

If you have always wanted to play famous pieces by the great composers, then, this book is for you. Let's get started on this exciting musical journey!

The Videos *Check out video*

This symbol means that there is a video lesson that corresponds to the material presented on the lesson page. These video lessons cover the concepts presented and also give instruction and tips on how to play certain pieces from the book.

To access the video lessons, go to steeplechasemusic.com. Click on the link at the top of the page for Piano Books. From the Piano Books webpage, click on the image for this book, *Piano Music Book of Bach Classics for Beginners.* On the webpage for *Piano Music Book of Bach Classics,* you will see a link to Video Lessons. Click that link for the Video Lessons webpage for this book. The video lessons are free. There is no limit on the number of times you may watch them.

Here is a list of some of the <u>Great</u> Pieces by J.S. Bach and other Famous Composers that you will learn in this book:

Beloved Pieces by J.S. Bach:

- *Aria from the Goldberg Variations*
- *Jesu, Joy of Man's Desiring*
- *Where Sheep Gently Graze*
- *Air on a G String*
- *Prelude in C Major from the Well-Tempered Clavier*
- *Toccata in D Minor (played in Phantom of the Opera)*
- *Invention in A Minor*
- *Minuet in G Major*
- *Musette in D Major*
- *March in G Major*
- *Minuet in C Minor*
- *Minuet in D Minor*
- *Musette in G Major*

Cherished Pieces by Bach's Contemporaries:

- Pachelbel's *Canon*
- Vivaldi's *Four Seasons*
- Handel's *Hallelujah*
- *Greensleeves*
- *Corelli's Gavotte in F Major*
- *Scarborough Fair*
- *Purcell's Minuet in A Minor*
- *Scarlatti's Aria*
- *Rameau's Rigaudon*

Table of Contents

Section 1: Introduction and Review of Basic Music Concepts

Page:

Section 2: Famous Pieces by J.S. Bach & Great Baroque Composers

Table of Contents for The Video Lessons

Important!

To access the video lessons, go to steeplechasemusic.com and click on the link at the top of the page for Piano Books. Then, from the Piano Books webpage, click on the image for this book, "Piano Music Book of Bach Classics". On the webpage for Piano Music Book of Bach Classics, you will see a link to Video Lessons. Click the link for the Video Lessons webpage for this book. The video lessons are free and there is no limit on the number of times you may watch them.

Bach Notes

Throughout this book, we will have sections called "Bach Notes". These sections are brief sketches from Bach's biography that will give you some insights into his life. Along with interesting facts about Bach, we will also have a few "side notes" that will focus on the lives of some of the other great Baroque composers whose music is featured in this book.

~ Bach's Early Years ~

J.S. Bach was born in east-central Germany on March 21, 1685 in Eisenach, Thuringia. Bach was born into a large extended family of musicians. As a matter of fact, Bach listed forty-two relatives who were musicians. From time to time, they would get together for family reunions. During these reunions, they would start by singing an opening chorale / hymn together. Then, they would dive into singing entertaining pieces, where they would harmonize and improvise on popular songs of the day. This style of improvised music is called "quodlibet" (meaning, what you like). With the Bach family, there was probably a lot of laughter involved on these occasions. Imagine having a family reunion where you all would sing and improvise on Taylor Swift or Michael Jackson songs.

From 1695 to 1699, Bach attended the Ohrdruf Lyceum, where he did very well in music and theology. As we know, these two subjects would be very important for the rest of his life. The young Bach had an excellent reputation as a singer, violinist, and keyboard player. From 1700 to 1707, was enrolled in the honors choir at the Church of Saint Michael in Lüneburg. At the Church of Saint Michael, he was able to study with some of the finest musicians in Lutheran Germany. It was at this time that Bach received his first professional position as the church organist at Arnstadt. At Arnstadt, he had with relatively light, work-related duties, a fairly generous salary, and a fine new organ tuned in a temperament that allowed him to perform music written in a wider range of musical keys. From 1700 to 1717, he was court composer at the Weimar court.

Getting Started

The inspiration for this book came from helping people who have dreamt of playing these famous pieces of classical music by Bach and other great composers from the period, but who haven't known where to begin. Over the last few decades of playing and teaching the piano, I have picked up a few helpful pointers that I would like to share with you at the beginning of the book:

1. One of the most important aspects for learning an instrument is cultivating a positive attitude. If you approach learning the piano with a happy, fun-loving spirit your mind and body will be much more receptive to learning new ideas. Having a can-do, positive outlook will not only make the process of learning more fun, but it has been proven to speed up the process of improving. So, you should always approach your piano playing as an exciting and rewarding activity of your day.

2. Another important aspect of playing the piano is forming good practice habits. Learning the piano is a fun and creative endeavor; if you develop good practice habits you will make rapid progress with your playing. This will require a little bit of focus and a proactive attitude on your part. However, it will make a big difference for you.

   Ideally, you should strive to practice around five to seven times per week (once per day) for about 20 to 40 minutes. If you have more time, that's great. However, it's best to spend your time practicing well (in an organized manner), rather than just spending a lot of time practicing. Along these lines, one of the most important facets of learning to play the piano is having some continuity in your practice routine. So, even on days that you are extremely busy, try to take 10-15 minutes to work on your piano playing. As best as you can, try to avoid missing more than three days of practicing in a row.

3. Have patience and a longterm perspective: You are embarking on a grand and lifelong adventure in music. Through this journey, you will discover new perspectives on sound, communication, friendship, success, coordination, self confidence, concentration, memory, and determination. For the most part, this learning will be a step-by-step process, where your ability and understanding of music will move ahead at a gradual pace. At other times, your progress may suddenly leap ahead to another level in a flash of inspiration.

Whatever your goals in music may be, it's best to cultivate an attitude that music is a lifelong journey and process of creating and developing. As an artist, you should continue to explore and develop your musical voice. Life will take you along different paths and these will be reflected in your music making. Enjoy this adventure, especially if you are just beginning. You are like some explorer stepping onto the deck of your ship heading out from your land's port to find yet-unexplored, new places. Enjoy the journey!

4. Lastly, a lot of beginning musicians overlook the importance of practicing with a metronome. A metronome is a mechanical or electronic device that keeps a steady beat. You can change the speed of the beats, which in music is called the "tempo", on all metronomes to allow for slower or faster pulses of rhythm.

As soon as possible, you should incorporate a metronome into your practicing for these piano pieces. This will help build and solidify your internal rhythm.

You can find a number of free or inexpensive metronome apps online. These will work on your computer, tablet, and smartphone. There are also a wide assortment of digital metronomes that you can purchase. Many of these can be found online or at your local music store for around ten dollars.

Damon Ferrante

GOOD NEWS: BONUS LESSONS!

This edition of *Piano Music Book of Bach Classics* includes free, bonus lessons.

1. Go to the Home Page of SteeplechaseMusic.com.

2. At the top of the Home Page, you will see a link for Piano Books.

3. Follow the link to the Piano Books webpage.

4. Then, click on the Cover / Link for *Piano Music Book of Bach Classics*.

5. Once you are on the webpage for *Piano Music Book of Bach Classics*, click MP3 Audio File Download and download the PDF and listen to the MP3 file.

Steeplechase Music Books

Also by Damon Ferrante

Piano Scales, Chords & Arpeggios Lessons with Elements of Basic Music Theory: Fun, Step-By-Step Guide for Beginner to Advanced Levels (Book & Videos)

Piano Book for Adult Beginners: Teach Yourself How to Play Famous Piano Songs, Read Music, Theory & Technique (Book & Streaming Videos)

Beginner Classical Piano Music: Teach Yourself How to Play Famous Pieces by Bach, Mozart, Beethoven & the Great Composers (Book, Streaming Videos & MP3 Audio)

Guitar Book for Adult Beginners: Teach Yourself How to Play Famous Guitar Songs, Guitar Chords, Music Theory & Technique (Book & Streaming Video Lessons)

Piano Book for Kids 5 & Up - Beginner Level: Learn to Play Famous Piano Songs, Easy Pieces & Fun Music, Technique & How to Read Music (Book & Streaming Video Lessons)

Guitar Book for Kids 5 & Up: Fun, Step-By-Step Songs & Lessons (Book & Videos)

Piano Music Book of Bach Classics for Beginners: Teach Yourself Famous Piano Solos & Easy Piano Sheet Music, Vivaldi, Handel, Music Theory, Chords, Scales, Exercises (Book & Streaming Video Lessons)

by Damon Ferrante

For additional information about music books, recordings, and concerts, please visit the Steeplechase website: www.steeplechasemusic.com

Steeplechase Arts

ISBN-13: 978-0-578-57653-4

Section 1:
Introduction &
Review of Basic
Music Concepts

Section 1: Introduction and Review of Basic Music Concepts

Section 1 of this book serves as a review of basic music and piano concepts or as an introduction to these ideas for readers who are just beginning to play the piano for the first time. The focus of Section 1, which is about thirty pages, is to present some of these beginner-level piano fundamentals, like the finger numbers, names of the notes, the treble and bass clefs, counting and rhythm, and playing with both hands. If you have some experience playing the piano already and can read music, you may want to glance over the lessons in this section as a brief review, before starting on Section 2: Famous Pieces by J.S. Bach & Great Baroque Composers. If you are new to the piano or are not familiar with these concepts, take your time with the lessons in Section 1; they will provide you with a good foundation for playing the music in Section 2.

Although there are some pieces of music in Section 1, the primary goal for this section is to refresh your memory about basic music concepts or introduce you to them, if you are new to the piano. Interspersed throughout Section 1, there are excerpts of famous pieces for the right hand, left hand, or hands together. There are also exercises to help you practice rhythm, counting, learning the notes on the keyboard, and playing with both hands at the same time. Some of the pieces included in Section 1 are easier versions of pieces that will also appear in Section 2.

The Video Lessons:

This symbol means that there is a video lesson that corresponds to the material presented on the lesson page. These video lessons cover the concepts presented and also give tips on how to play certain famous pieces from the book.

To access the video lessons, go to steeplechasemusic.com and click on the link at the top of the page for Piano Books. Then, from the Piano Books webpage, click on the image for this book, *Piano Music Book of Bach Classics*. On the webpage for *Piano Music Book of Bach Classics*, you will see a link to Video Lessons. Click the link for the Video Lessons webpage for this book. The video lessons are free and there is no limit on the number of times you may watch them.

Getting Started: An Overview of the Notes on the Keyboard

- The White Keys on the piano follow an alphabetic pattern that goes from A to G. In other words, this is the pattern: A, B, C, D, E, F, G.
- This pattern starts at the bottom (low bass notes) of the piano keyboard and repeats many times as the notes go upward and get higher in pitch ("sound").
- With your RH ("Right Hand") Index Finger, find the "A" key just 2 keys below MIddle C (See the Chart below). Move your Index Finger up (to the right) one key at a time. Try saying the letters as you press down each key.

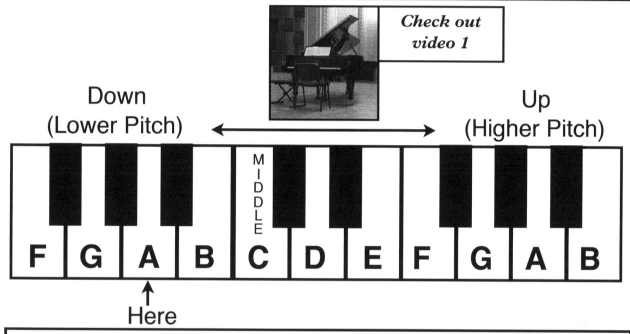

Check out video 1

Down (Lower Pitch) ← → Up (Higher Pitch)

Here

- It is a good idea to associate each key with some object and imagine the object on top of the key. This will help you remember the name and location of each key.
- For this exercise, let's image that the piano keyboard is a table with food on it. The food, on this imagined table, will be placed in a set order going from left to right (See the chart below). Find the key "A" below Middle C and name the foods as you move upward (right). When you get to the second key "A", the pattern will repeat. Repeat this exercise.

White Keys Exercise: A= Apple, B= Bread, C= Cheese, D= Dessert, E= Eggs, F= Fish, G= Grapes

Exercises:
- Try Locating Middle C with Finger #1 (Thumb) of your Right Hand (RH)
- Try Locating Middle C with Finger #1 (Thumb) of your Left Hand (LH)
- Try Locating D with Finger #2 (Pointer Finger) of your Right Hand (RH)
- Try Locating E with Finger #3 (Middle Finger) of your Right Hand (RH)

An Overview of Hand Position & Finger Numbers

- To create a good hand position for piano playing is easy. With both hands, imagine that you are holding an apple (with your palms facing upward and your fingers curved). Then, turn your palms to the floor and keep your fingers curved. **See Video Lesson 1**
- For piano playing, our fingers are given numbers. The numbers are the same for both hands. **See Video Lesson 1**

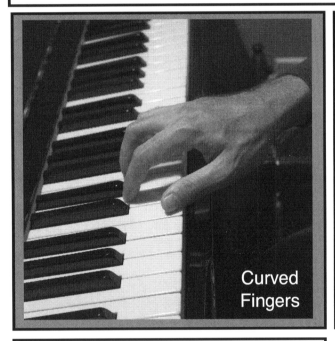

Curved Fingers

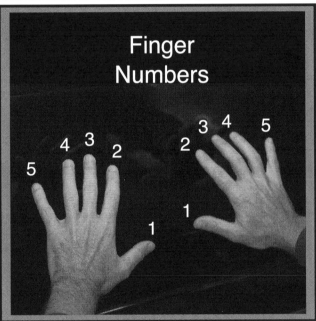

Finger Numbers

- RH stands for Right Hand.
- LH stands for Left Hand.

Finger Numbers
- Thumb = Finger #1
- Pointer = Finger #2
- Middle = Finger #3
- Ring = Finger #4
- Pinky = Finger #5

The finger numbers are the same for both hands. For example, the thumb is finger #1 in both the right hand and left hand and the pinky is finger #5 in both hands.

For Video Lesson 1, go to www.steeplechasemusic.com.

An Overview of Counting and Measures

- Music is composed of groups of beats called measures.
- Measures are set off by vertical lines, called bar lines.
- Measures most commonly contain 2, 3, or 4 beats.
- Below, are examples of sets of four measures in 4/4 time.
- In 4/4 time, you will count 4 beats for each measure.
  In other words, you will count: 1234, 1234, 1234, 1234.
- Try counting aloud and clapping the beats for the exercise below.

Check out video 2

Example 1:

| 1 2 3 4 | 1 2 3 4 | 1 2 3 4 | 1 2 3 4 ‖

Example 2:
Try Clapping on the X: On the First Beat.

| 1 2 3 4 | 1 2 3 4 | 1 2 3 4 | 1 2 3 4 ‖
  X   X   X   X

Example 3:
Try Clapping on the X: On the First and Third Beats.

| 1 2 3 4 | 1 2 3 4 | 1 2 3 4 | 1 2 3 4 ‖
  X   X   X   X   X   X   X   X

Example 4:
Try Clapping on the X: On the Second Beat.

| 1 2 3 4 | 1 2 3 4 | 1 2 3 4 | 1 2 3 4 ‖
    X   X   X   X

Three-Note Exercises: Using the Right Hand ("RH")

• Try these exercises, which use the notes C, D, and E in the right hand ("RH").
• In your right hand, use Thumb for Middle C, use Pointer for D, and use Middle Finger for E.
• Take a look at the keyboard chart and photo below and practice each one 5-10 times.
• As an extra bonus, try saying the letter names aloud as you play each exercise.
  This will help you associate the note name with the key and finger number.

RH

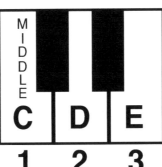

Notes: C   D   E
Finger Numbers: **1   2   3**

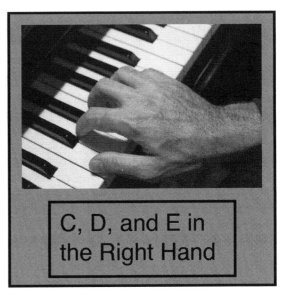

C, D, and E in the Right Hand

Exercise #1

RH: **1 1 1 1** | **2 2 2 2** | **3 3 3 3** | **2 2 1 1** ‖
      C C C C | D D D D | E E E E | D D C C

Exercise #2

RH: **1 1 2 2** | **1 1 3 3** | **1 1 2 2** | **1 1 1 1** ‖
      C C D D | C C E E | C C D D | C C C C

Five-Note Pieces as Studies for the Right Hand (RH)

- Here are a few more pieces that use the five fingers of the right hand.
- Remember to find Middle C with the Thumb of your right hand (RH).

RH

Notes: **C D E F G**

Finger Numbers: **1 2 3 4 5**

New Notes

Exercise #1

The numbers here are for <u>beats</u>, not fingers. When there is a blank space, don't play for that beat or beats.

Beats:	1	2	3	4	1	2	3	4	1	2	3	4	1	2	3	4
	F	E	D	C	G	G	G	G	F	E	D	C	G	G	C	C

Ode to Joy

We will learn a more advanced version of Beethoven's *Ode to Joy*, later in this book.

Beats:	1	2	3	4	1	2	3	4	1	2	3	4	1	2	3	4
	E	E	F	G	G	F	E	D	C	C	D	E	E	D	D	

Beats:	1	2	3	4	1	2	3	4	1	2	3	4	1	2	3	4
	E	E	F	G	G	F	E	D	C	C	D	E	D	C	C	

17

Three-Note Exercises: Studies for the Left Hand ("LH")

- Try these exercises, which use the notes A, B, and Middle C in the left hand ("LH").
- In your left hand, use Thumb for Middle C, use Pointer for B, and use Middle Finger for A.
- Take a look at the keyboard chart and photo below and practice each one 5-10 times.
- As an extra bonus, try saying the letter names aloud as you play each exercise.
  This will help you associate the note name with the key and finger number. **Have Fun!**

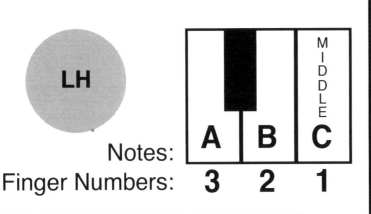

LH

Notes: | A | B | C (MIDDLE)

Finger Numbers: **3** **2** **1**

The numbers here are for <u>fingers</u>, not beats.

A, B, and C in the Left Hand

Exercise #1

LH: **1 1 2 3** | **1 1 2 3** | **2 2 3 3** | **2 2 3 3** ‖
    C C B A | **C C B A** | **B B A A** | **B B A A**

Exercise #2

LH: **3 2 1 2** | **3 2 1 2** | **1 1 3 3** | **1 2 3 3** ‖
    A B C B | **A B C B** | **C C A A** | **C B A A**

18

An Overview of Time Signatures

- Measures are composed of groups of beats called Time Signatures or Meter (both terms mean the same thing and are interchangeable).
- The most common Time Signatures (or "meters") are groups of 2, 3, or 4 beats per measure: 2/4, 3/4, and 4/4 Time Signatures.
- 2/4 Time Signature groups the notes into measures of 2 beats. Count: "One,Two" for each measure.
- 3/4 Time Signature groups the notes into measures of 3 beats. Count: "One,Two,Three" for each measure.
- 4/4 Time Signature groups the notes into measures of 4 beats. Count: "One,Two,Three, Four" for each measure.
- Below, are examples of sets of 4 measures in 2/4, 3/4, and 4/4.
- Count aloud and clap on the first beat for the exercises below.

Check out video 3

Example 1: 2/4 Time Signature
Try Clapping on the X: On the First Beat.

2/4

| 1 | 2 | | 1 | 2 | | 1 | 2 | | 1 | 2 |
| X | | | X | | | X | | | X | |

Example 2: 3/4 Time Signature
Try Clapping on the X: On the First Beat.

3/4

| 1 | 2 | 3 | | 1 | 2 | 3 | | 1 | 2 | 3 | | 1 | 2 | 3 |
| X | | | | X | | | | X | | | | X | | |

Example 3: 4/4 Time Signature
Try Clapping on the X: On the First Beat.

4/4

| 1 | 2 | 3 | 4 | | 1 | 2 | 3 | 4 | | 1 | 2 | 3 | 4 | | 1 | 2 | 3 | 4 |
| X | | | | | X | | | | | X | | | | | X | | | |

Putting Both Hands Together Using the Keyboard Notes: A,B,C,D & E

• Here are 2 pieces for both hands. They use the notes A, B, C, D, and E.
• The numbers listed are for the <u>beats</u>, not the finger numbers.
• If there is a blank space, don't play for that beat or beats.
• Both Thumbs will share Middle C.

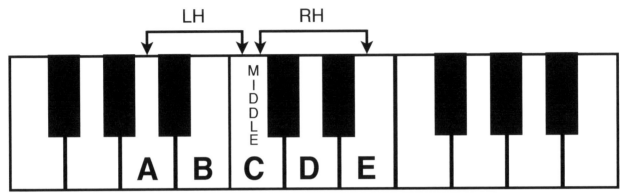

Finger
Numbers: **3   2   1   2   3**

Both Thumbs (RH and LH) share Middle C.

Beethoven 5th Symphony Theme

	RH:	E	E	E	C			D	D	D			
3	Beats:	1	2	3	1	2	3	1	2	3	1	2	3
4	LH:										B		

We will learn a more advanced version of Beethoven's 5th *Symphony Theme,* later in this book.

Study for Both Hands

	RH:	C	D	E	C			C	D	E	G		C
3	Beats:	1	2	3	1	2	3	1	2	3	1	2	3
4	LH:					G	G						G

Mozart's Twinkle, Twinkle, Little Star with Both Hands: G,A,B,C,D,E & F

> • If you see a blank space, don't play for that beat or beats.
> • Remember to place both of your thumbs on Middle C.

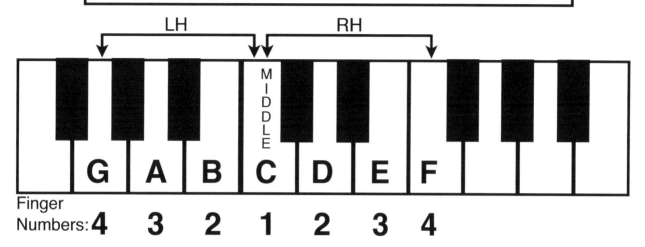

Twinkle, Twinkle, Little Star

> • Try to count the beats aloud, while you play.

4/4

RH:	D D	E E D	C C	
Beats: 1 2 3 4	1 2 3 4	1 2 3 4	1 2 3 4
LH: G G		B B	A A G

RH: D D C C		D D C C	
Beats: 1 2 3 4	1 2 3 4	1 2 3 4	1 2 3 4
LH:	B B A		B B A

RH:	D D	E E D	C C	
Beats: 1 2 3 4	1 2 3 4	1 2 3 4	1 2 3 4
LH: G G		B B	A A G

Music Theory:
An Overview of Intervals

- In music, the distance between any 2 notes is called an "Interval".
- Intervals can be played at the same time, for example, if you press down two piano keys or they can be played one after the other, for example, if you play the note "C" and then the note "D".
- On the piano, the easiest way to understand intervals is to look at the keyboard. Play Middle C with your Left-Hand Index Finger, then play D with your Right-Hand Index finger. This interval is called a 2nd.
- Next, play Middle C with your Left-Hand Index Finger, then play E with your Right-Hand Index finger. This interval is called a 3rd.
- Follow these steps in the 2 diagrams below. Use the Left-Hand Index Finger when you see LH and use the Right-Hand Index Finger when you see RH.

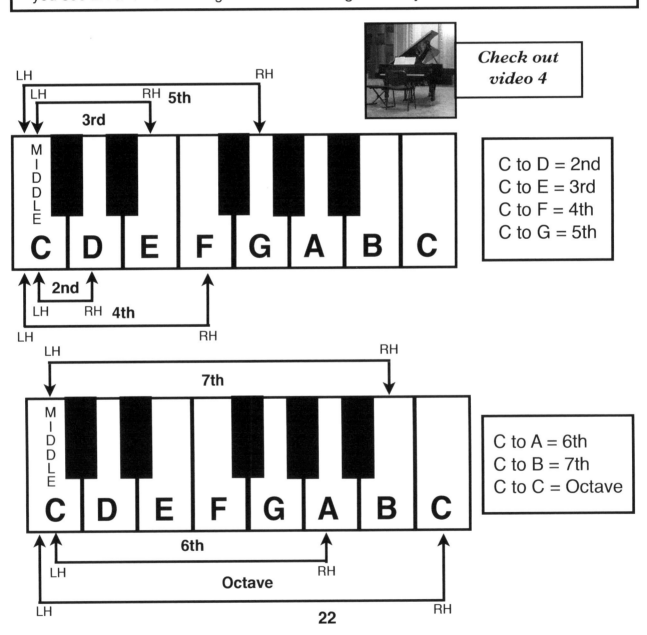

Check out video 4

C to D = 2nd
C to E = 3rd
C to F = 4th
C to G = 5th

C to A = 6th
C to B = 7th
C to C = Octave

Basic Rhythms: Whole Notes, Half Notes & Quarter Notes

- Let's take a look at some basic rhythms.
- Quarter Notes are notes that get 1 Beat (or Count).
- Half Notes are notes that get 2 Beats (or Counts).
- Whole Notes are notes that get 4 Beats (or Counts).
- In the next 3 examples, try counting on each beat of the 4/4 measures aloud, for example: 1,2,3,4.
- Clap on the quarter, half, and whole notes.

Check out video 5

♩ = 1 Beat   ♩ = 2 Beats   𝅝 = 4 Beats

Example 1:
Try Clapping on each "X", while counting the beats.

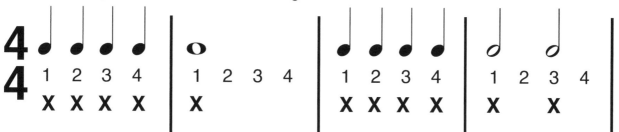

Example 2:
Try Clapping on each "X", while counting the beats.

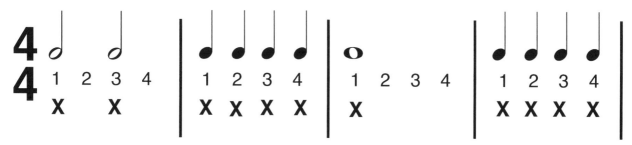

Example 3:
Try Clapping on each "X", while counting the beats.

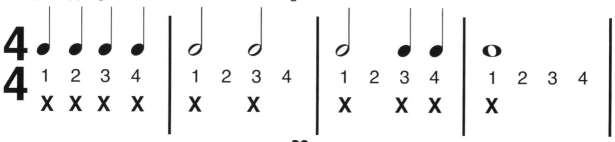

Treble Clef Notes: Middle C, D & E

- The Treble Clef mainly is used for notes above Middle C.
- About 90% of the time, it is used for the Right Hand.
  (There are a few occasions in songs or pieces when it is used for the Left Hand.)
- The Treble Clef is made up of Lines and Spaces that correspond to keys on the piano.
  Each Line or Space is linked to <u>one</u> (and only one) key on the piano.
- We will learn more about the lines and spaces of the Treble Clef in the following lessons.

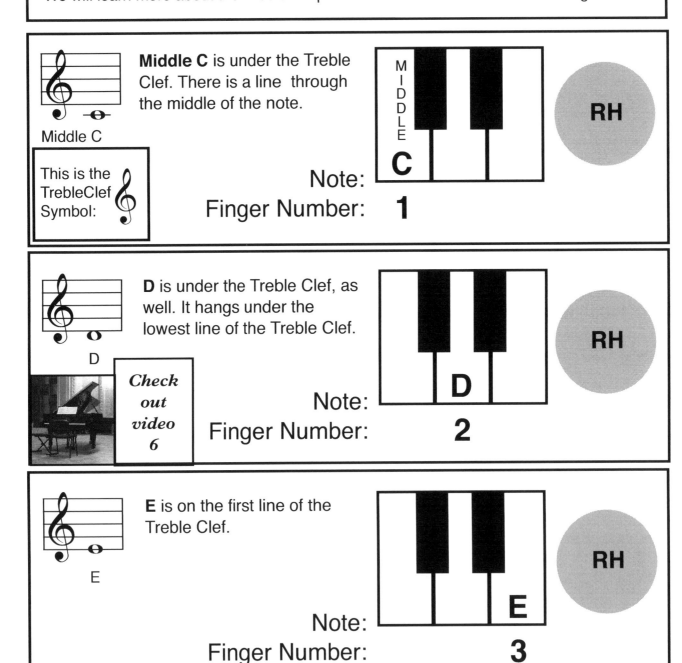

Middle C

Middle C is under the Treble Clef. There is a line through the middle of the note.

This is the TrebleClef Symbol:

Note: C

Finger Number: 1

RH

D

D is under the Treble Clef, as well. It hangs under the lowest line of the Treble Clef.

Check out video 6

Note: D

Finger Number: 2

RH

E

E is on the first line of the Treble Clef.

Note: E

Finger Number: 3

RH

Treble Clef Exercises: Middle C, D & E (RH)

- Let's play 4 exercises with notes of the Treble Clef: C, D, and E.
- Remember to find Middle C with the Thumb of your right hand (RH).

Notes:

Finger Numbers:

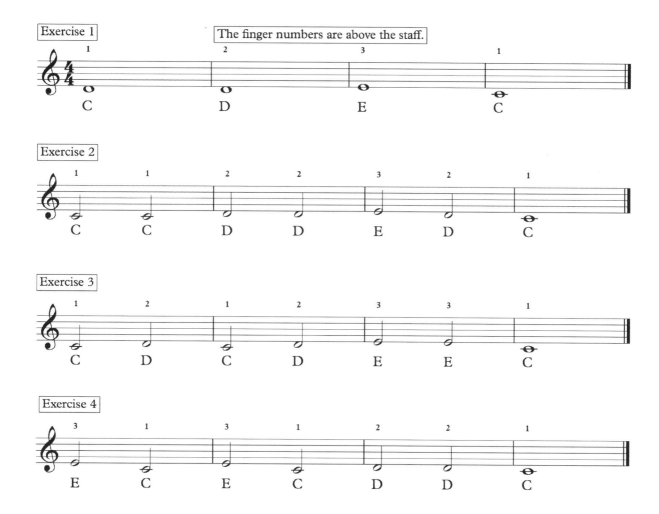

More Treble Clef Exercises: Middle C, D, E & F (RH)

- Let's add the note F, which is on the 1st space of the Treble Clef.
- Remember to find Middle C with the Thumb of your right hand (RH).

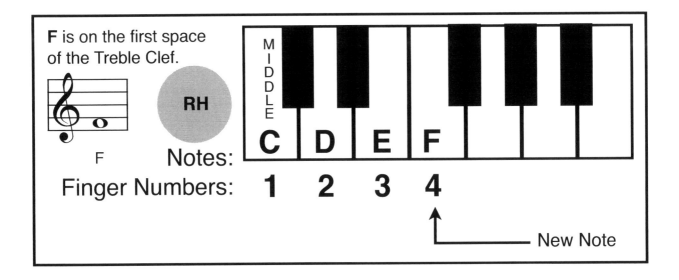

F is on the first space of the Treble Clef.

F

RH

Notes: C D E F

Finger Numbers: 1 2 3 4

New Note

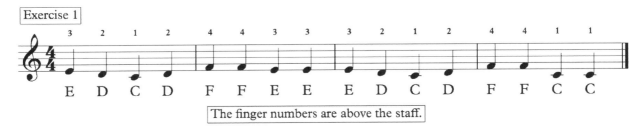

Exercise 1

3 2 1 2 4 4 3 3 3 2 1 2 4 4 1 1

E D C D F F E E E D C D F F C C

The finger numbers are above the staff.

Exercise 2

1 3 2 4 3 2 1 2 2 1

C E D F E D C D D C

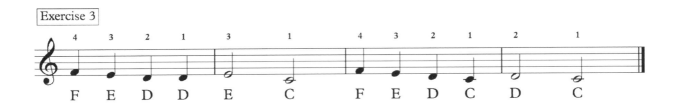

Exercise 3

4 3 2 1 3 1 4 3 2 1 2 1

F E D D E C F E D C D C

26

Treble Clef Lines: Overview

- Each line of the Treble Clef stands for a specific note and key on the piano.
- The lines have numbers that go from 1 to 5. Line 1 is the lowest line. Line 5 is the top line (or highest line) on the Treble Clef.
- To help you remember the note names of each line, memorize the saying below. In the saying ("Every Good Bird Does Fly"). "Every" stands for "E", "Good" stands for "G", "Bird" stands for "B", "Does" stands for "D", and "Fly" stands for "F".
- The "E" of "Every" stands for the "E" piano key 2 notes above Middle C. See the charts below to better understand these notes.

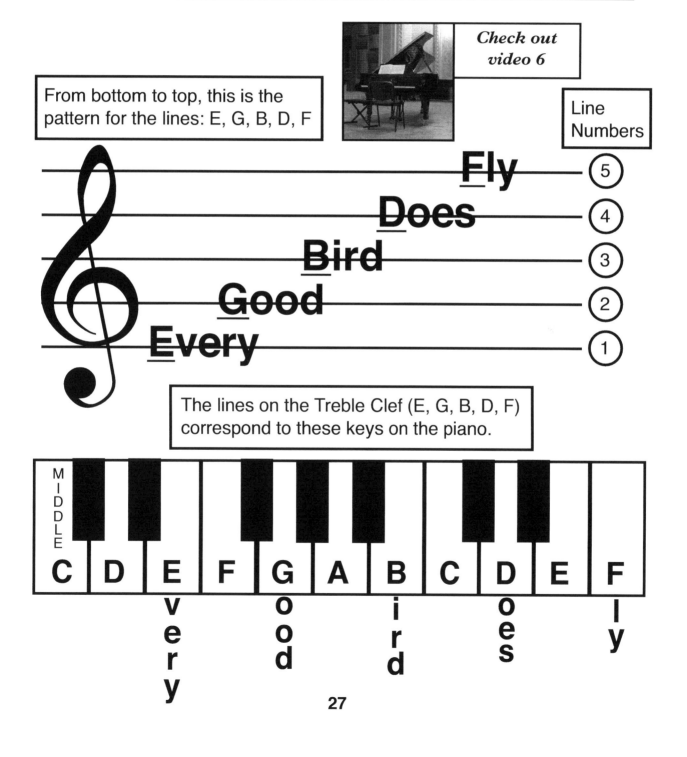

Check out video 6

From bottom to top, this is the pattern for the lines: E, G, B, D, F

Line Numbers

Fly — ⑤
Does — ④
Bird — ③
Good — ②
Every — ①

The lines on the Treble Clef (E, G, B, D, F) correspond to these keys on the piano.

MIDDLE C | D | E | F | G | A | B | C | D | E | F
very / ood / ird / oes / ly

Treble Clef Spaces: Overview

- Each space of the Treble Clef stands for a specific note and key on the piano.
- The spaces have numbers that go from 1 to 4. Space 1 is the lowest space. Space 4 is the top space (or highest space) on the Treble Clef.
- To help you learn the note names of each space, remember that the spaces of the Treble Clef form the word "Face" spelled upside down (from bottom space to top.)
- The "F" of "Face" stands for the "F" piano key 4 notes above Middle C.
- See the charts below to better understand the other notes.

Check out video 6

From bottom to top, this is the pattern for the Spaces: F, A, C, E

Space Numbers

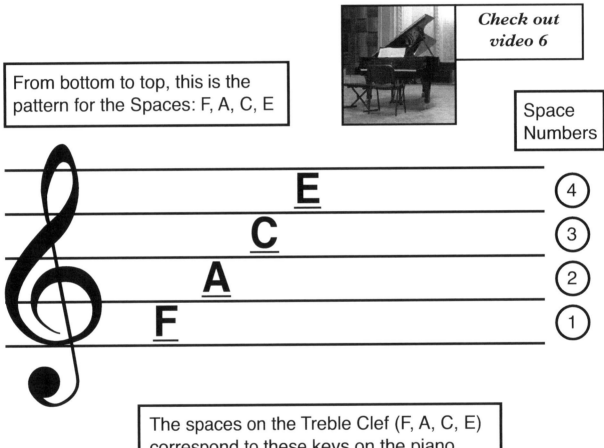

The spaces on the Treble Clef (F, A, C, E) correspond to these keys on the piano.

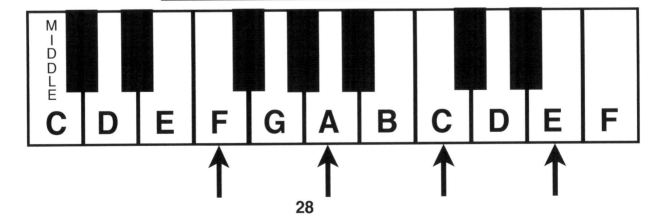

Bass Clef Notes: Middle C, B & A

- The Bass Clef mainly is used for notes below Middle C.
- About 90% of the time, it is used for the Left Hand.
  (There are a few occasions in pieces when it is used for the Right Hand.)
- The word "Bass" is pronounced like the word "Base" (as in "Baseball").
- The Bass Clef is made up of Lines and Spaces that correspond to keys on the piano.
  Each Line or Space is linked to <u>one</u> (and only one) key on the piano.
- We will learn more about the lines and spaces of the Bass Clef in the following lessons.

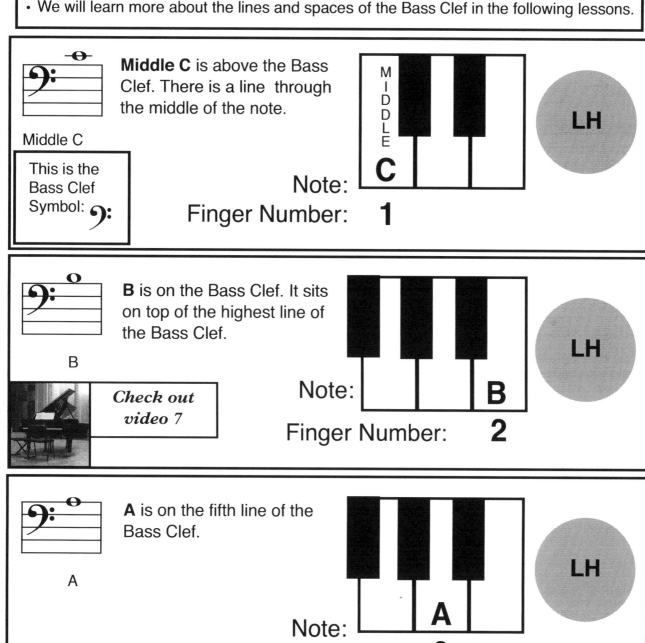

Middle C

Middle C is above the Bass Clef. There is a line through the middle of the note.

This is the Bass Clef Symbol: 𝄢

Note:
Finger Number: **1**

B

B is on the Bass Clef. It sits on top of the highest line of the Bass Clef.

Check out video 7

Note:
Finger Number: **2**

A

A is on the fifth line of the Bass Clef.

Note:
Finger Number: **3**

Bass Clef Exercises:
A, B & Middle C

- Let's play 4 exercises with notes of the Bass Clef: A, B, and C.
- Remember to find Middle C with the Thumb of your left hand (LH).

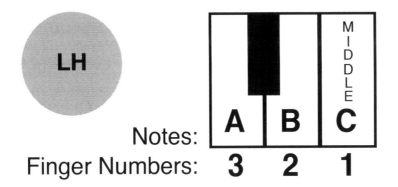

LH

Notes:
Finger Numbers:

MIDDLE

A   B   C

3   2   1

Try saying the notes aloud as you play each exercise.

The numbers here are for <u>fingers</u>, not beats.

Bass Clef Lines: Overview

- Each line of the Bass Clef stands for a specific note and key on the piano.
- The lines have numbers that go from 1 to 5. Line 1 is the lowest line. Line 5 is the top line (or highest line) on the Bass Clef.
- To help you remember the note names of each line, memorize the saying below. In the saying ("Good Baked Desserts For All"). "Good" stands for "G", "Baked" stands for "B", "Desserts" stands for "D", "For" stands for "F", and "All" stands for "A".
- The "A" of "All" stands for the "A" piano key two notes below Middle C. See the charts below to better understand these notes.

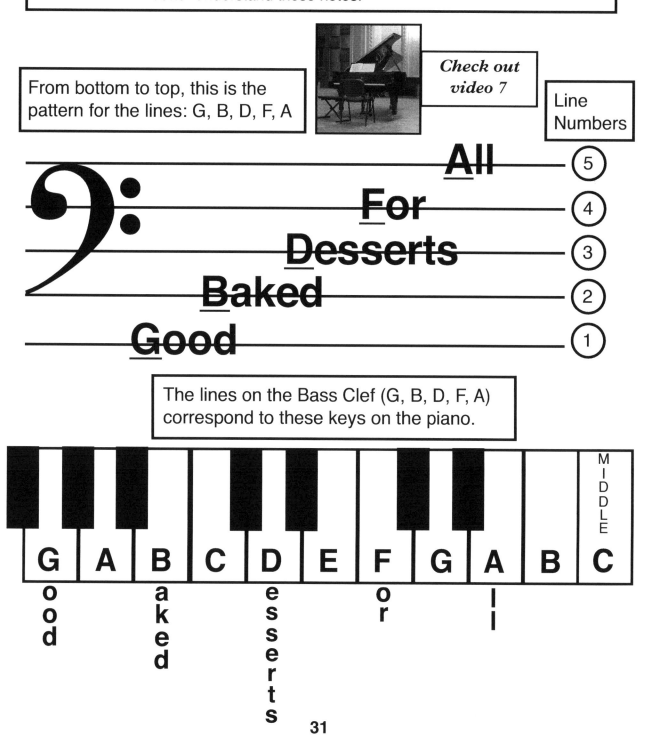

From bottom to top, this is the pattern for the lines: G, B, D, F, A

Check out video 7

Line Numbers

All — ⑤
For — ④
Desserts — ③
Baked — ②
Good — ①

The lines on the Bass Clef (G, B, D, F, A) correspond to these keys on the piano.

| G | A | B | C | D | E | F | G | A | B | C |
| o o d | | a k e d | | e s s e r t s | | o r | | l l | | MIDDLE |

31

Bass Clef Spaces: Overview

- Each space of the Bass Clef stands for a specific note and key on the piano.
- The spaces have numbers that go from 1 to 4. Space 1 is the lowest space. Space 4 is the top space (or highest space) on the Bass Clef.
- To help you learn the note names of each space, remember that the spaces of the Bass Clef form the phrase "All cows eat grass".
- The word "All" stands for the key and note "A"; the word "Cows" stands for "C".
- See the charts below to better understand the other notes.

Check out video 7

Space Numbers

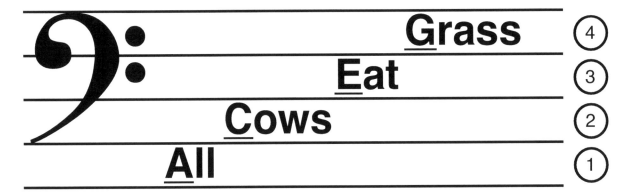

Grass ④

Eat ③

Cows ②

All ①

The spaces on the Bass Clef (A, C, E, G) correspond to these keys on the piano.

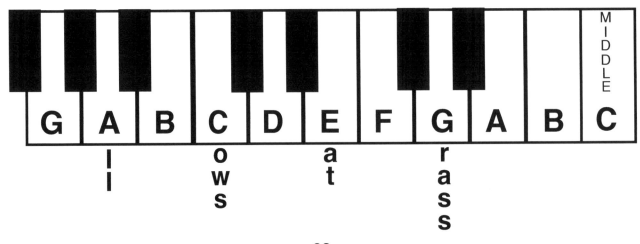

32

Easy Left-Hand Chords: C Major, F Major & G7

- Chords are 3 or more notes played at the same time.
- In order to play chords well, keep your fingers curved for the notes that you play and lift your fingers that are not being used for the chord.
- Take a look at video lesson 8 to see and hear how these techniques work.
- For these chords, use the Left Hand (LH).
- We are going to look at 3 chords in this lesson.

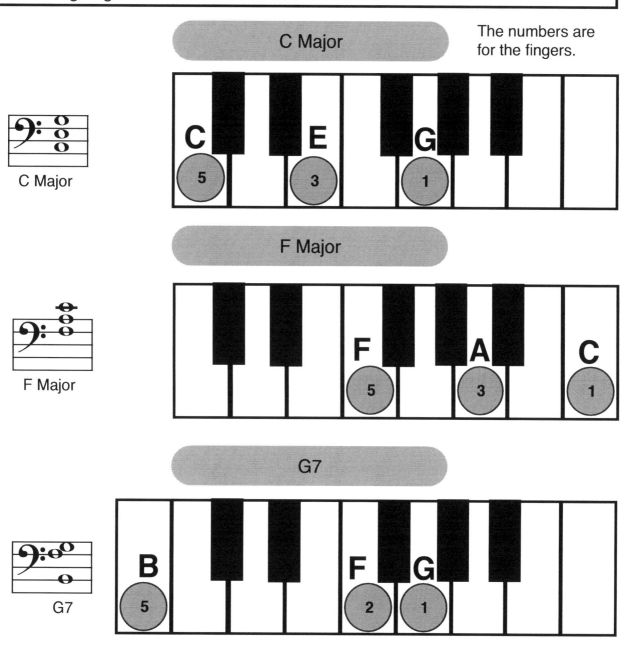

More Easy Left-Hand Chords
A Minor, D Minor & G Major

- Let's look at 3 more chords for the Left Hand: A Minor, D Minor, & G Major.
- Make sure to keep your fingers curved and lift the fingers that do not play.

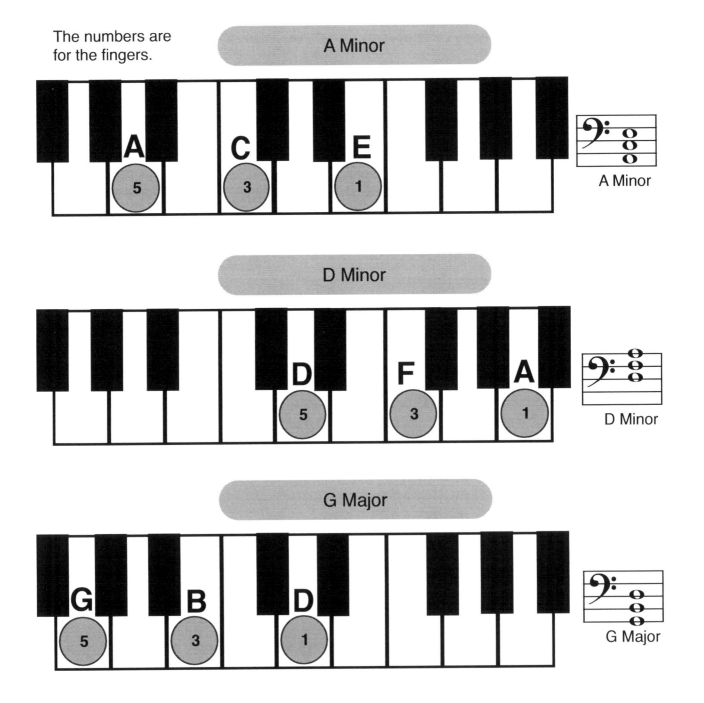

The numbers are for the fingers.

A Minor

A Minor

D Minor

D Minor

G Major

G Major

Left-Hand Chord Studies

In this lesson, we are going to practice playing some of the chords from the previous two lessons. With each of these exercises, take your time to master the transition from one chord to the next. Building up this kind of left-hand coordination will greatly help you, once we start learning the pieces from the next section of the book. If you have a metronome, you might set it to quarter note equals 60 (in other words sixty beats per minute) for this exercise. As a side note, there are many free metronome apps available online. If you have a smart phone, tablet, computer, or similar electronic device, you might take a moment to find a free metronome app for it online; you can use a metronome to help you learn the pieces later in the book.

When you move from one chord to the next, try to form the new chord with your fingers, before playing the keys. This technique will improve your muscle memory for the chords. Along these lines, try to avoid sliding your fingers along the keyboard to find the notes of the chords. This will not only hamper the development of your muscle memory for playing chords, but it will also make it more likely that you will play a few wrong notes.

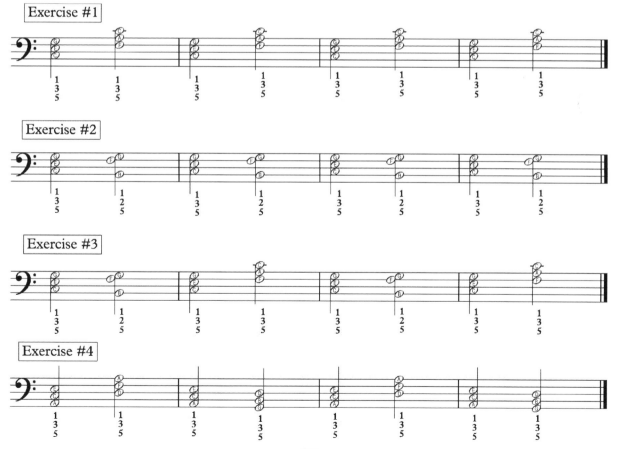

The Grand Staff: Overview

- The Grand Staff is formed by combining the Treble and Bass Clefs.
- All of the rules that we have learned so far about both clefs are still true for the Grand Staff. Using the Grand Staff makes it easier to read music written for both hands.
- Study the chart below to understand how the Staff works.

See Video Lesson 8

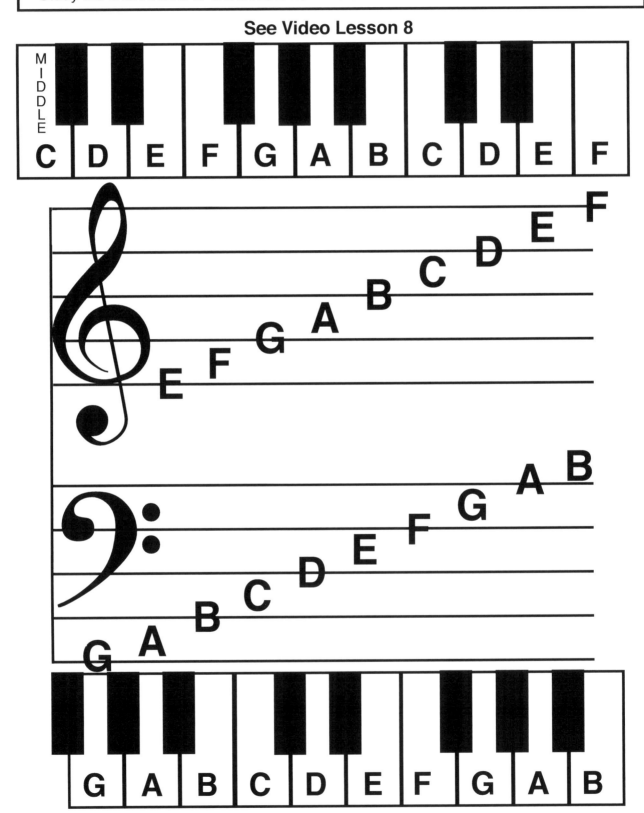

Naming the Notes on the Grand Staff

For this lesson, let's try naming the notes on the grand staff below. Remember to use your note-name sayings from earlier in the book. You may also refer back to the grand staff on the previous page. Try naming the notes for one measure, then go back and repeat naming the notes for that measure three times. Once you feel confident about the note names, go on to the next measure. After you have finished naming the notes on the entire page, go back to the beginning of the lesson and slowly play each note on the piano. You might also say the note aloud as you play it. This will begin to reinforce your understanding of the notes on the page and the keys on the piano keyboard.

Music Theory:
What are Sharps & Flats?

Check Out Video 9

- On the piano, there are two types of keys: Black Keys and White Keys.
- The White Keys stand for natural notes, for example, C, D, E, F, G, A and B.
- The Black Keys (also called "accidentals") stand for Sharp or Flat Notes.
- Sharp Notes use this symbol: #
- Flat Notes use this symbol: ♭
- Here are some examples of Sharp Notes: F#, G#, A#, C#, D#
- Here are some examples of Flat Notes: Gb, Ab, Bb, Db, Eb

- On the piano keyboard, Sharp Keys are located directly to the right of their corresponding Natural Key (White Key). For example, F Sharp (F#) is the next key to the right from F (also called "F Natural"). C Sharp (C#) is the black key directly to the right of C (also called "C Natural").
- This pattern, of going to the next key directly to the right, holds true for all of the sharp notes going up and down the piano keyboard.
- Using the chart below, try locating the following sharp keys on the piano: C#, F#, D#, A#, G#.

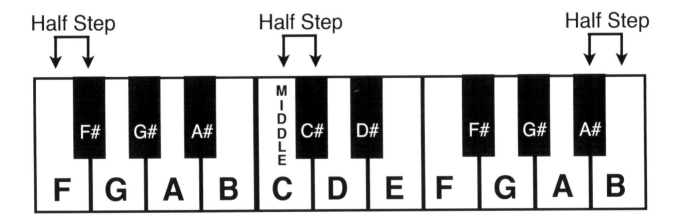

The distance from a White Key to a Black Key, for example, F to F#, C to C#, or A# to B, is called a **Half Step** or Minor Second. **Remember this.** It is a bit of important information we will be referring to many times in the next book.

38

Music Theory: More on Sharps and Flats

- On the piano keyboard, Flat Keys are located directly to the left of their corresponding Natural Key (White Key). For example, G Flat (Gb) is the next black key to the left from G (also called "G Natural"). E Flat (Eb) is the black key directly to the left of E (also called "E Natural").
- This pattern, of going to the next key directly to the left, holds true for all of the flat notes going up and down the piano keyboard.
- Using the chart below, try locating the following flat keys on the piano: Ab, Db, Gb, Eb, Bb. **Remember: This pattern is the same for the entire keyboard.**

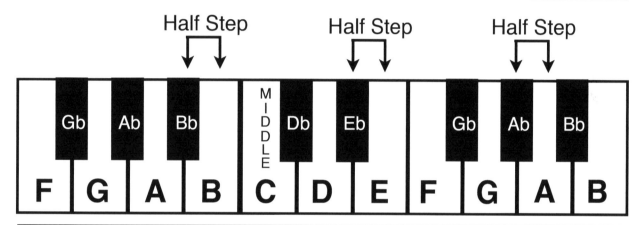

- The distance (up or down) from a White Key to a Black Key, for example, from B to Bb, Eb to E, or A to Ab, is called a Half Step or Minor Second. See Above.

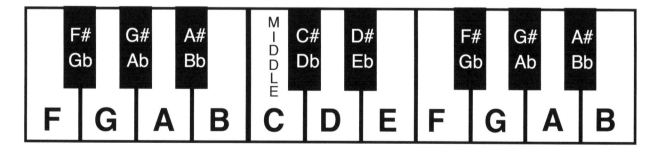

- You might have noticed in the last two lessons that there are 2 names for each Black Key: A Sharp Name and a Flat Name. This is true for the entire piano.
- Depending on the musical context (which we will learn more about throughout this book), a black key may be called by either its sharp or flat name. For example, A Flat and G Sharp are the same key on the piano; C Sharp and D Flat are the same key; and F Sharp and G Flat are the same key. See Above.

Scarborough Fair

- *Scarborough Fair* is in 3/4 time. Count: "One, Two, Three" for each measure.
- Place your left-hand thumb on middle C and your right-hand thumb on the D, which is located next to middle C on the right-hand side.
- For the F#, play the black key directly to the right of F on the piano.

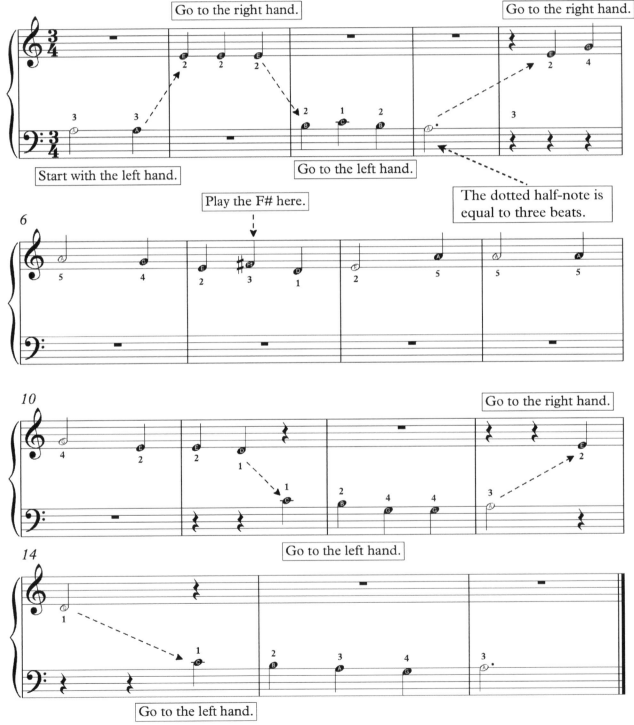

Section 2:
Famous Pieces by J.S. Bach &
Great Baroque Composers

J.S. Bach was primarily known as a virtuoso organist, rather than as a composer during his life. He is one of the towering geniuses of music. His sacred music, organ pieces, choral works, and instrumental music display immense originality, technique, and intelligence. His musical language is unique, expansive, and shows great variety, in terms of style and ideas. The music that he wrote is among the most cherished in history.

Now we are ready to start learning some great pieces by Bach and other wonderful composers from the Baroque Period!

Throughout Section 2, we will go over strategies that will make learning each piece easier for you, as well as some additional, fundamental musical concepts. Here are some of the concepts and techniques that you will learn, along with the pieces, in this section of the book:

• dynamics

• crescendo and diminuendo markings

• dotted notes

• subdividing

• coordinating both hands

• counting beats

• reading in both clefs

• slurs: phase markers

• left-hand accompaniment styles

• upbeats

• thumb-under technique

Remember, you can listen to a recording of all the pieces in the book by going to steeplechasemusic.com and listening to the free MP3 audio file from the book's webpage. Enjoy!

March in G Major: Overview & Lesson

March in G Major is a wonderful piece by Bach to get us started on our musical journey. The piece has a robust character, which is energized by the use of eighth notes in the melody in measure fourteen. Eighth notes are equal to half of a quarter note and are counted as half of a beat.

They look like this:

In a measure of 4/4 time, eight eighth notes would be counted like this: 1 &, 2 &, 3 &, 4 &. The "&" stands for the word "and". The "&" or "and" is the halfway point of a beat. See the example below:

Musicians often refer the the halfway point of a beat as the "and". For example, a musician might say, "play it on the *and* of *two*". This would mean: play it at the halfway point between beats two and three. Try to find it in the above example.

When you divide a beat into sections, it is called "subdividing". Let's practice counting and playing groups of eighth notes and quarter notes. Use middle C. Remember to subdivide the eighth notes: for example, 1 &, 2 &, 3 &, 4 &.

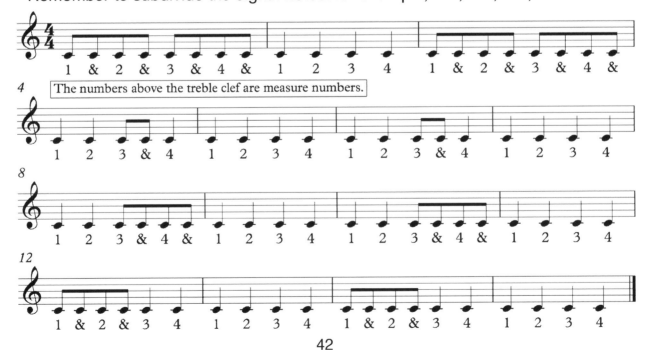

42

Music Theory: An Overview of Dynamics

Before we start our first piece by Bach, let's look at a music concept that will help you play the pieces that make up the collection of music in the rest of this book.

Dynamics is a term that we use for the loudness and softness of the notes in music. In pieces and songs, you will see dynamic indications represented as letters (F, P, MP, or MF, for example). These letters are abbreviations for Italian words.

p stands for the term "piano", which means soft (like a whisper, but not the quietest whisper).

mp stands for the term "mezzo-piano", which means medium soft (like a quiet conversation).

mf stands for the term "mezzo-forte", which means medium loud (like a normal conversation).

f stands for the term "forte", which means loud (like a shout).

Dynamics are a relative concept in music. In other words, you might consider that each piece has a slightly different range from soft to loud. Forte ("loud") in the context of a Vivaldi piece may be a little different than forte in a Bach piece. So, let's think of dynamics as a general concept that varies slightly from piece to piece. Part of what makes music so exciting and inspiring is finding the nuance and detail in the poetics of each piece. Exploring dynamics on the piano, along with many other musical concepts, will be a big part of this book.

In piano sheet music (sometimes called the "score"), we are given indications on how to make the music gradually louder or softer. In a lighthearted way, you might think of this as the piano version of turning up or turning down the volume on a car stereo, TV, or an audio device. In piano music we use two symbols:

Crescendo means to get gradually louder

Diminuendo means to get gradually quieter

March in G Major: Tutorial

As we prepare for playing our first piece by Bach, let's look at some common techniques that will occur in many of the pieces in this book. Remember to take a look at the video lesson to better understand these two piano techniques.

Check Out Video 10

Shifting Hand Positions: The first technique we will practice is shifting hand positions. Since there are eighty-eight keys on the piano and we have only five fingers on each hand, from time to time when playing pieces, we will need to spread our fingers and also shift our hand position along the piano keyboard.

Example 1 starts on measure five in Bach's *March in G Major.* There are three hand position shifts: One starts on the second beat of the first measure; one starts on the second beat of the second measure; and one starts on the first beat of the fourth measure. Each of these position shifts is numbered and marked by brackets. For the first two of these position shifts, gently spread your fingers as you are playing to position your hand for each note. For the third position shift, we will use the finger-over technique (described below).

Try playing the notes of position 1 a few times. Once you feel comfortable playing position 1, try playing the melody notes of position 2. Then, once you feel comfortable playing the position 2, put both position 1 and position 2 together. Play them slowly, at first.

Finger-Over Technique / Thumb-Under Technique: Since we only have five fingers and many melodies and musical phrases on the piano use more than five notes, we need to shift our fingers over the thumb or move our thumb under the fingers. This is called the "finger-over" or "thumb-under" technique. (Please take a moment to look at the video lesson.)

Take a look at the last note (the E) of measure three below and the first note (the D) of measure four. Do you see how the E is played with finger number one and the D is played with finger number four? To play these two notes in succession and to connect the melody line, you will need to gently move your fourth finger over your thumb. Give this a try.

The numbers under the notes are beats.

Example 2 starts on measure 29 of the *March in G Major.* To change positions, your thumb will go under your third finger on the fourth note. Try playing the first four notes several times.

March in G Major

J.S. Bach

This piece is in the key of G major. This means that any F note that you see in the music will be an F#.

Always try to use the same finger numbers. If you play with the same finger numbers each time, you will speed up your learning of the music.

The dots above or below the notes indicate staccato, which means detached or bouncy sounding notes.

In music, look for repeating notes and patterns, for example the G notes in the first four measures of the piece. If you group these repeated notes as a musical idea in your mind, rather than four unrelated G notes, it will be easier to learn and remember the music in this section. This principle holds true for patterns in music, in other words, keep on the "lookout" for them.

RH 4th finger over thumb.

Music Theory Concept → The curved lines above or below two or more different notes are called slurs or phrase markers. They indicate that you should play in a smooth manner. They also indicate the beginning and end of a musical phrase.

Sharps and flats carry over to the same notes in the same measure, for example C# in measure 14.

Remember to subdivide the eighth notes.

The two lines and two dots (in the last measure of this page) are a repeat sign. This indicates to go back to the beginning of the piece, where there is another repeat sign, and play the first page one more time. Then, continue to the next page.

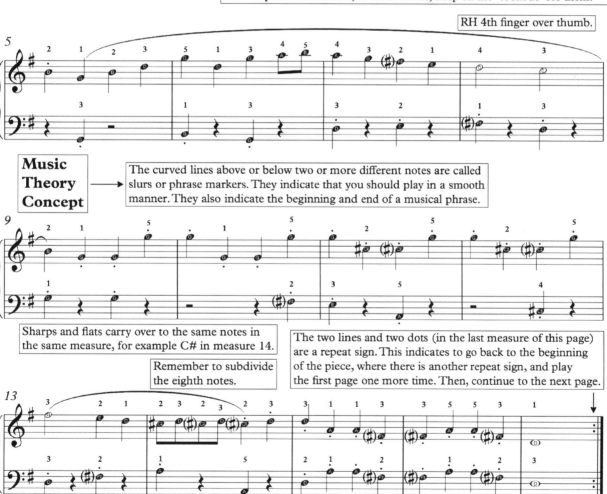

Remember, you can download and listen to a recording of all the pieces in the book by going to steeplechasemusic.com and downloading the free MP3 audio file from the book's webpage.

45

There is another repeat sign at the end of this piece. Please play the second page one more time. By the way, repeat signs are a common feature in music from the Baroque period. (You will see more of them throughout this book.)

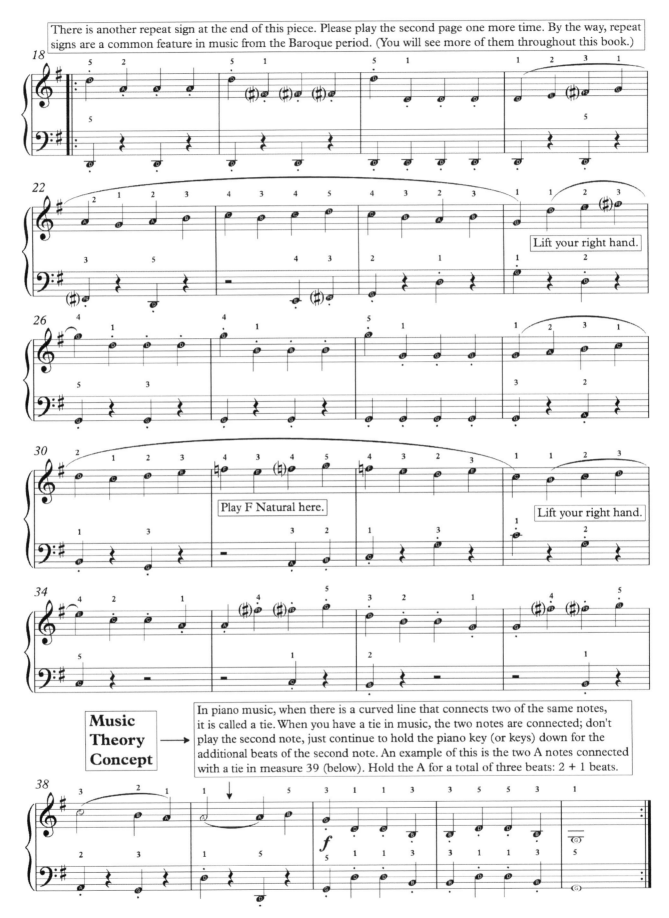

Play F Natural here.

Lift your right hand.

Music Theory Concept → In piano music, when there is a curved line that connects two of the same notes, it is called a tie. When you have a tie in music, the two notes are connected; don't play the second note, just continue to hold the piano key (or keys) down for the additional beats of the second note. An example of this is the two A notes connected with a tie in measure 39 (below). Hold the A for a total of three beats: 2 + 1 beats.

46

Throughout Section 2 of the book, we will go over strategies that will make learning each piece easier for you. As we are getting started, I would like to mention one approach that will greatly aid in your learning these pieces.

Try this: Focus on learning only one or two measures at a time, starting with the right hand, then the left hand, and, finally, when you have mastered playing the music for each hand separately, play both hands together. Then, repeat this process for learning the next measure or two measures of the piece. This approach will greatly speed up your learning. It will also make your playing of the pieces much more secure. Please focus on this approach in your practice sessions, rather than only playing the piece from beginning to end.

Minuet in G Major

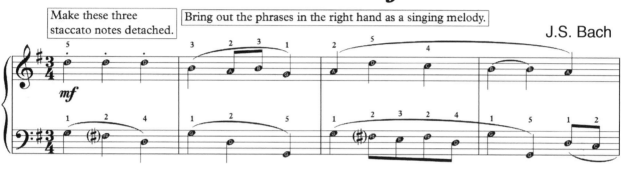

J.S. Bach

Make these three staccato notes detached.

Bring out the phrases in the right hand as a singing melody.

Remember that the key of G major has an F# instead of an F Natural.

Try to feel the distance of the octave between your left-hand thumb and pinky, as you play the notes in this measure.

For this measure, count: 1, 2 &, 3 &.

For this measure, count: 1, 2, 3 &. Also, remember that the RH note B is tied.

These two measures are sequences: patterns that repeat on different notes. Bach uses this compositional technique in a number of ingenious ways. Keep an eye and ear out for sequences; they occur in a number of pieces in this book.

Remember that we have two F# notes in this measure.

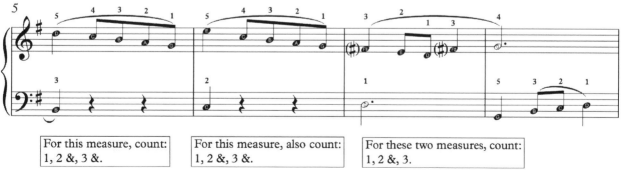

For this measure, count: 1, 2 &, 3 &.

For this measure, also count: 1, 2 &, 3 &.

For these two measures, count: 1, 2 &, 3.

* By the way, in this book, we will be learning three pieces, which are all called "Minuet in G Major". They are three different pieces. As you learn more of Bach's music, you will discover that he wasn't into fancy titles for pieces. He names his instrumental music, typically, "March in C", "Prelude in F", "Fugue in D Minor", etc.

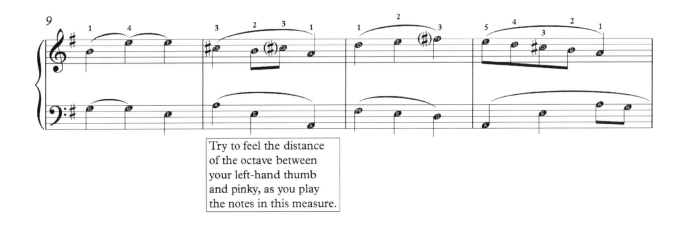

Try to feel the distance
of the octave between
your left-hand thumb
and pinky, as you play
the notes in this measure.

These two measures are also sequences.

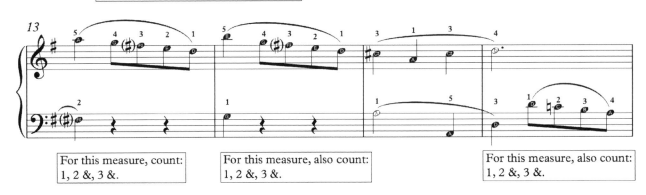

For this measure, count:
1, 2 &, 3 &.

For this measure, also count:
1, 2 &, 3 &.

For this measure, also count:
1, 2 &, 3 &.

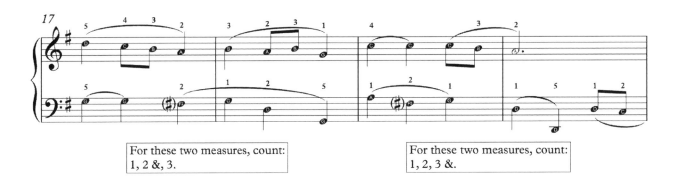

For these two measures, count:
1, 2 &, 3.

For these two measures, count:
1, 2, 3 &.

Remember that we have two
F# notes in this measure.

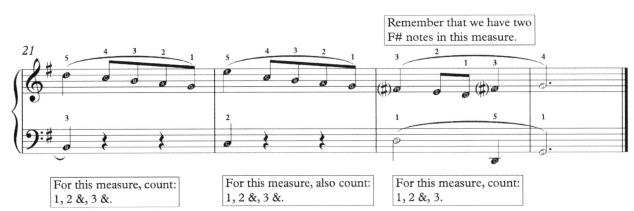

For this measure, count:
1, 2 &, 3 &.

For this measure, also count:
1, 2 &, 3 &.

For this measure, count:
1, 2, 3.

Toccata in D Minor

Performance Note: In this famous and dramatic piece by Bach, you will play a number of sharps and flats: the black keys on the piano. The piece, originally composed for pipe organ, is arranged here for easy piano. It contains a number of dissonant notes (the musical equivalent of hot peppers and spices used in cooking, to borrow a culinary analogy). These dissonant notes build up the musical tension in the piece. Please be aware of the tension and release in the music. ***Enjoy!***

The RH index finger goes over the thumb here.

Check out Video 11

Left Hand for this measure.

Right Hand for this measure.

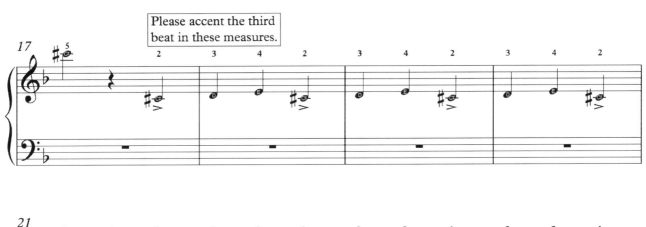

Please accent the third
beat in these measures.

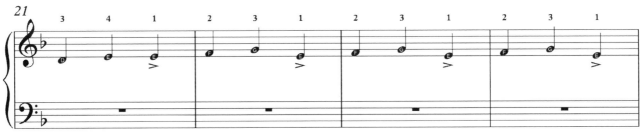

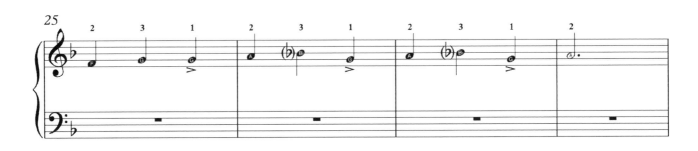

Please accent the third
beat in these measures.

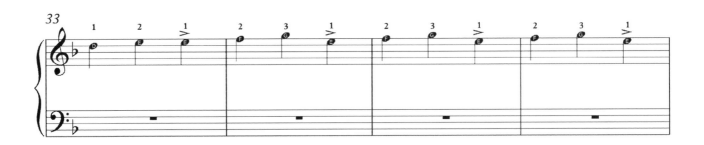

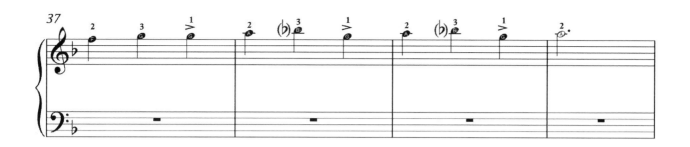

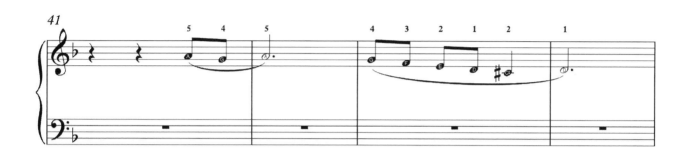

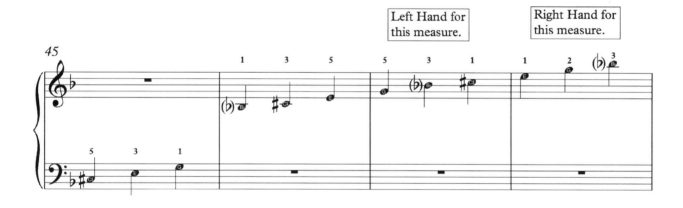

Left Hand for this measure.

Right Hand for this measure.

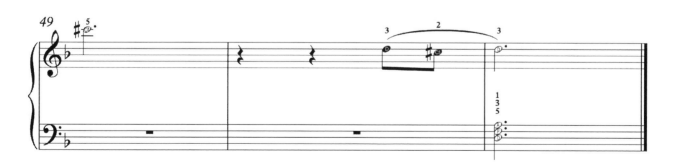

What a great piece of music!

Spring
(from the Four Seasons)

Antonio Vivaldi

This piece starts with an upbeat: The note Middle C. An upbeat is a note (or notes) that occurs before the first full measure. The upbeat leads into the beginning of the music. For this upbeat, count: 1, 2, 3, 4. Start on beat 4.

Practice right hand alone, while counting the beats. Then, practice left hand alone, while counting the beats. Then, put both hands together. Play quite slowly at first. Then, gradually speed up the tempo (the time).

Tie these two notes.

Tie these two chords.

Tie these
two notes.

Tie these
two chords.

Tie these
two chords.

Tie these
two chords.

Music Theory:
Sixteenth Notes

Sixteenth notes are equal to one fourth of a quarter note. In other words, you need four sixteenth notes to equal one quarter note. Sixteenth notes have two beams (or flags); this distinguishes them from other notes, like eighth notes, which have one beam (or flag).

In the following exercises, we are going to practice the most common combinations for sixteenth notes. For the purposes of these exercises, we are only playing the notes on middle C.

In the first exercise, let's play and count four quarter notes and then play and count groups of four sixteenth notes. When we count groups of four sixteenth notes, we say, "1 e & a". The first number of each group indicates the beat. For example, the "2" in "2 e & a" indicates the second beat of the measure. The "3" in "3 e & a" indicates the third beat of the measure. The "4" in "4 e & a" indicates the fourth beat.

In the second exercise, let's play and count four quarter notes and then play and count groups of four eighth notes and sixteenth notes.

In the third exercise, let's play and count four quarter notes and then play and count another combination of groups of four eighth notes and sixteenth notes.

In the fourth exercise, let's play and count four quarter notes and then play and count groups of four dotted-eighth notes and sixteenth notes.

54

Where Sheep Gently Graze

This wonderful and lyrical piece introduces a few sixteenth notes in the 3rd system (starting in measure 9). Before you start playing the notes on the piano, go to the 3rd system (starting in measure nine) and clap and say the rhythm. Try this also for the 4th system.

The piece is in 2/4 time signature. There are two beats in each measure. *Enjoy!*

J.S. Bach

First, practice the right hand part for each phrase (marked by the slur above the notes). Then, play the left hand alone. Then, put both hands together. Do this for each phrase, one at a time. Remember to count the beats and subdivide for each.

Autumn

(from the Four Seasons)

In this next, famous piece by Vivaldi, there are a number of repeated musical patterns. While you are learning the music, pay attention to these patterns; being aware of them will greatly help you in learning the piece at a faster pace and in a more secure manner.

Antonio Vivaldi

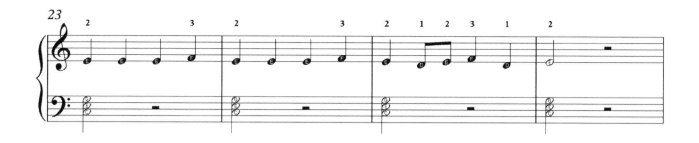

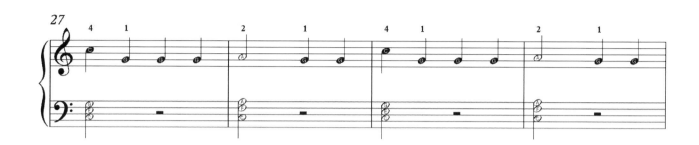

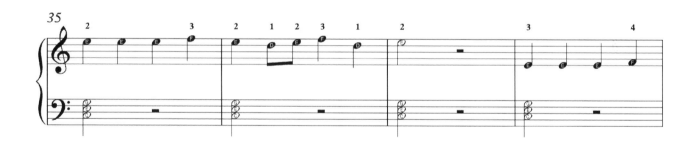

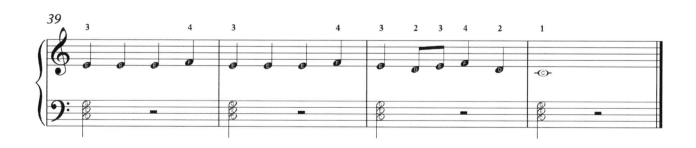

Minuet in G Minor

This is an excellent piece by Bach. The G Minor key gives it a bit of a mysterious sound. It is in the time signature of 3/4 and has a number of Bb and Eb notes. As a side note, later on in the book, we will learn another piece that is also called "Minuet in G Minor".

Andante

J.S. Bach

These three measures are sequences: the same pattern played on different notes.

These two measures are sequences.

Keep a close eye on the crescendo and diminuendo marks, which, respectively,
indicate to get gradually louder or softer. They bring out a lot of character in the music.

Bring out the contrasting sounds between legato (smooth) notes and staccato (detached) notes.

Drop the right-hand wrist
for the first note of each
two-note group in this bar.

Check Out Video 13

Air

In learning this outstanding piece by Henry Purcell, it would be best to practice each one-measure phrase first in the right hand, then in the left hand, and, then, with both hands together. Proceed this way through the piece and you will learn it at a fast pace.

Henry Purcell

Air on a G String

Here is an easy-piano arrangement of one of the famous and sublime pieces by Bach.
Enjoy!

J.S. Bach

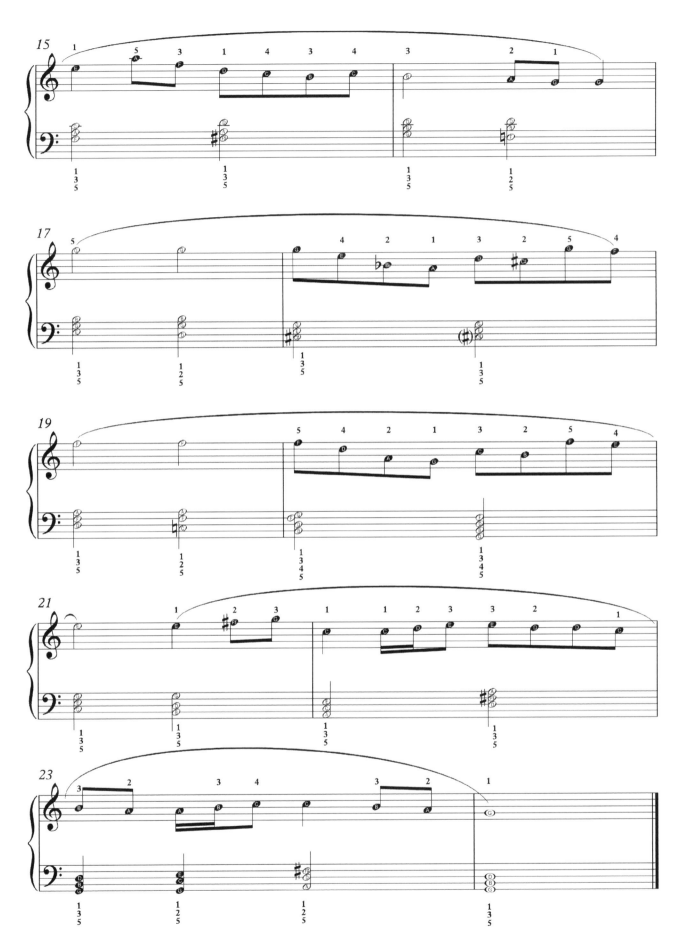

Music Theory: Dotted Notes & Rests

Dotted Notes: In the upcoming pieces, we are going to see a number of dotted notes: notes with a dot place on the right-hand side of the note head:

In music this dot adds half the value to the note's duration. For example, a quarter note, which is equal to 1 beat in 2/4, 3/4, and 4/4 time, would be equal to 1 1/2 beats if we added a dot. A dotted half-note would be equal to three beats: 2 beats + 1 beat extra for the dot. Try this example below and play along with counting. Do you hear the effect of the dotted note? It gives a little emphasis off of the beat. This is called syncopation.

1 2 3 4   1 2 & 3 4   1 2 3 4 & 1 2 3 4

Count the beats aloud while playing Middle C.

Rests: Another element of music that we will be seeing in upcoming pieces are rests. Rests indicate silences in music. They are very important in giving the music shape. Often times, they are overlooked by beginning pianists. Here are some examples:

This measure contains a whole rest. This rest counts for four beats. Also, the rest often fills an entire measure. In piano music, it is sometimes used to indicate that one hand will not be playing for a period of time or that an entire measure is silent.

This measure contains two half rests. These rests count for two beats of silence in a measure. For these examples, try counting in your head, while moving your eyes along the page to follow the motion of the beat. This will help you develop a sense of the proportions of each different rest.

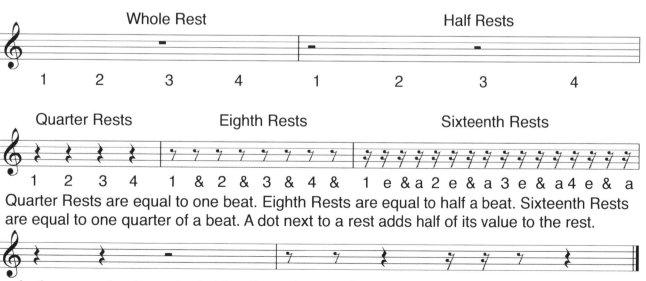

Quarter Rests are equal to one beat. Eighth Rests are equal to half a beat. Sixteenth Rests are equal to one quarter of a beat. A dot next to a rest adds half of its value to the rest.

In the example above, try to identify each type of rest.

Aria

Georg Philipp Telemann

Here we have a lyrical aria by the great Telemann. Try bringing out the melody in the right hand and follow the crescendo and diminuendo marks. These will help evoke the vocal quality of the melody. Also, make the left hand softer than the right hand; this will help to create the operatic and emotional shape of the melody and accompaniment in each hand.

Here we have an example of a dotted quarter note.

Count:

1   2   &

Jesu, Joy of Man's Desiring

Congratulations on your progress to this point in the book! You are now developing a good repertoire of famous pieces that you can play for your family, friends, and yourself.

This next piece is one of Bach's hauntingly beautiful melodies. Like the Telemann aria that we just learned, the right-hand melody should be a little louder than the left-hand chord accompaniment.

J.S. Bach

Most of the LH chord fingerings are 1, 3, 5.

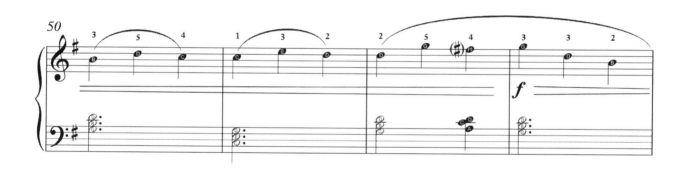

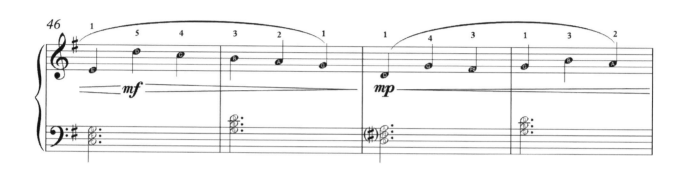

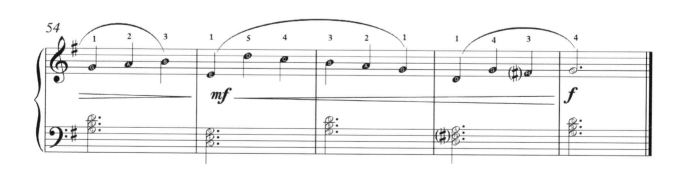

Gavotte in F

This delightful piece is a "conversation" between the right and left hands. Have fun exploring the interplay of each pianistic voice.

< : This is an accent symbol. It indicates that we should give a particular note or chord a little more emphasis. To get an accent on the piano play the key or keys a little faster and louder. The accents in the piece oftentimes come at the end of a measure (on the fourth beat) and serve as upbeats, propelling the music into the downbeat (the first beat) of the next measure.

Arcangelo Corelli

Prelude in C Major: Tutorial

In this lesson, we are going to prepare for playing the *C Major Prelude* by J.S. Bach. Arpeggios are one of the key concepts at work in this piece. The term "arpeggio" comes from the Italian word "arpa", which means "harp". Along these lines, an arpeggio is a chord played one note at a time, instead of a chord where all of the notes are played at once. This style of playing one note at a time mimics the sound of a harp.

Let's start by playing the first eight measures as chords, rather than arpeggios. Once you are comfortable with the fingering, try playing the first four measures as arpeggios (one note at a time). This method of reducing the arpeggios to block chords can be done for the entire piece and will make it easier to learn.

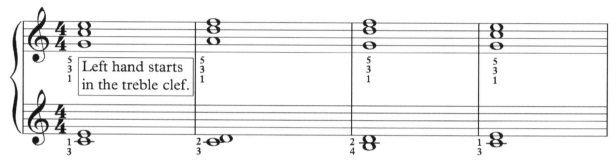

Once you are comfortable playing the block chords, try playing the arpeggios (below). Keep the muscle memory of the block chords in your mind while playing the arpeggios.

Prelude in C Major

See Video Lesson 14

Adagio — Try to bring out the top note of each measure.

J.S. Bach

Left hand starts in the treble clef.

This measure has the same fingering as the previous one. This two-measure pattern occurs for the whole piece.

These two measures are the same as the first two in the piece. They act as a kind of "little ending", before the music moves in a different harmonic direction.

These are high A notes.

The F# repeats in this measure.

The F# repeats in this measure too.

This is the B
below middle C.

The F# repeats
in this measure.

This is the A
below middle C.

This is the A
below middle C.

The left hand will go into
the bass clef in this measure.

Slow down a little bit in the last two measures.
This will indicate that the piece is ending.

Purcell Minuet:
Tutorial

A minuet is a stately dance form in 3/4 time. When you play a minuet, take a moderate tempo: not too fast and not too slow. In exercise one, let's practice the first four measures of Purcell's minuet in the right hand.

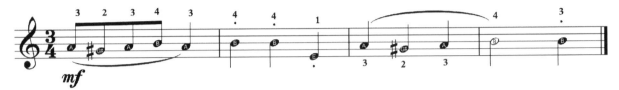

Now, in exercise two, let's practice the first four measures of the left hand.

For exercise three, let's put both hands together. Practice this slowly, at first. It is all right if you would like to practice and each measure by repeating the measure several times.

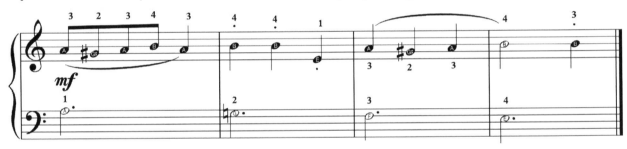

In exercise four, let's work on the right-hand part for the second system of music. You might notice that there are some similar patterns between exercises one and four.

For exercise five, let's put both hands together.

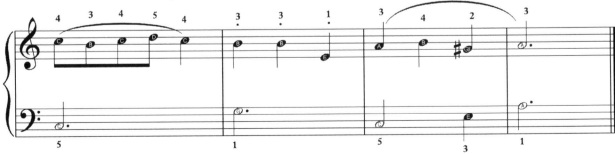

Minuet

Andante

Henry Purcell

Musette in G

Here is another beautiful piece by Bach. It is meant to be played in a moderate tempo: think "walking pace". There are a few hand-position shifts, as well as a number of F# notes. Please take your time and learn the music in sections. **Have fun!**

J.S. Bach

Aria from the Goldberg Variations

Here we have the sublime aria from the *Goldberg Variations* by J.S. Bach. It is in a very slow tempo. Learn each phrase, one at a time: left hand, then right hand. Memorize the finger numbers; this will help you learn the piece a bit faster. If you have a metronome, use it to keep a steady 3/4 beat. Take your time. Have fun! This is a great piece.

J.S. Bach

Greensleeves: Tutorial

In exercise one, we are going to look a the left-hand technique for *Greensleeves*. Most of the left-hand sections outline chords, played one note at a time. These are called "arpeggios" in music terminology. The word "arpeggio" is Italian and means harp. So, when you are playing this preliminary exercise, try to imagine the piano sounding a little bit like a harp. If possible, let your left-hand wrist drop down a little bit at the beginning of each measure. At the end of each measure, let it raise back to its normal position: parallel to the left hand.

In exercise two, we are going to focus on the rhythm for the melody in the right hand. We are going to exclude all of the notes of the melody, except for "D". As you take a look at the rhythm for the melody of *Greensleeves,* you will notice that it is in 3/4 time (that is, three quarter notes or their equivalent in each measure) and composed of half notes, quarter notes, eighth notes, and dotted-quarter notes. The dotted quarter notes are equal to one and a half beats. You should count them like this: 1&2. Take a moment to find the note "D" with your right hand thumb and try the exercise. Remember to count the beats and subdivisions (the sections marked between each beat).

Now, in exercise three, let's try playing the right-hand melody of the opening. Please use (and even memorize) the fingering that is listed. As a general guideline, it's best to always strive to use the same fingering once you learn a piece of music. This way, your mind will not have to constantly be figuring out which fingers to place on the keys.

In exercise four, let's take a look at another section of the melody in the right hand. You might notice that the index finger will move over the thumb in measure two. As well, please notice the dynamics: forte down to mezzopiano. This means that it will go from loud (relative to the overall sound of the piece) down to fairly soft. When you are playing the piece, starting on the next page, try to make the right hand a little bit louder than the left. This will balance the sound of the piece and bring out the melody.

Greensleeves

Play the left-hand part softer than the right-hand part.

Little Prelude
in G Major

J.S. Bach

Remember that the note F is F# in this piece.

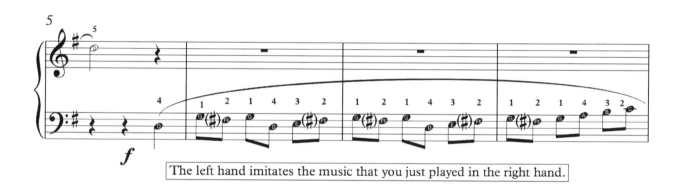

The left hand imitates the music that you just played in the right hand.

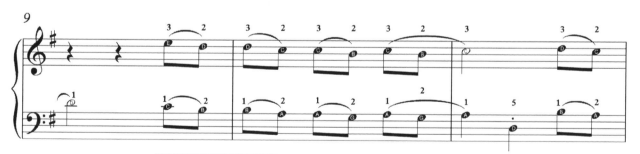

Drop and lift your wrist with each two-note group.

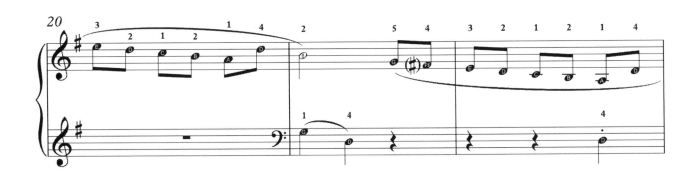

Drop and lift your wrist with each two-note group.

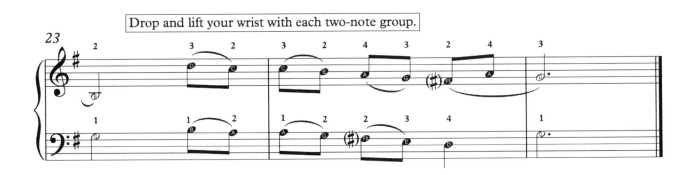

Minuet in D Minor

J.S. Bach

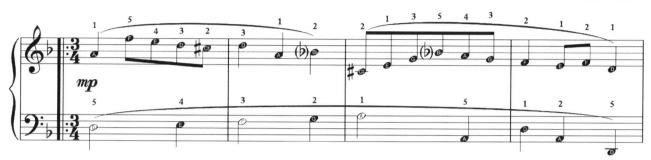

D minor has a Bb in the key signature. When you see a "B" in the music, make sure to play a Bb.

This symbol is called the first repeat. When you reach the end of this measure, go back to the beginning of the piece. When you arrive at this measure a second time, skip it and go to the second repeat.

This measure is the second repeat.

Make sure to play a B natural, not a Bb in this measure.

March in D Major

This wonderful march is in the key of D Major, which has two sharp notes: F# and C#. Please pay attention to the F# and C# notes. If you don't play them, the music will sound a bit funny.

J.S. Bach

Remember F# & C# in this piece by Bach.

Minuet in G Major

This is our second *Minuet in G Major* by Bach. It's a famous piece that has been played by thousands of pianists. "Andante" is a tempo indication. It means to play at a moderate, "walking" pace. When you are playing the piece, try to bring out the interplay between the two hands. **Have Fun!**

Check Out Video 15

Andante

J.S. Bach

Bring out the contrasting sounds between legato (smooth) notes and staccato (detached) notes.

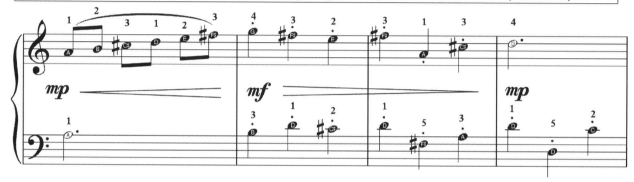

Drop the right-hand wrist
for the first note of each
three-note group in these bars.

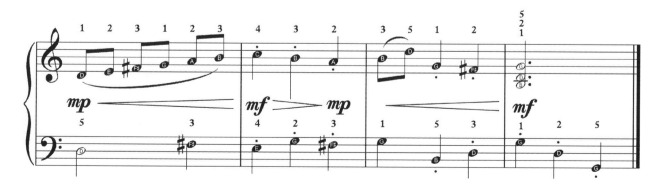

Minuet in G Minor

Here we have our second *Minuet in G Minor* by J.S. Bach. It is a moving piece that shows great compositional skill for both the right and left hands.

The Minuet was an elegant couples dance that was popular in aristocratic European ballrooms, especially in France and England, from around 1650 to 1750. Bach, like many of the other composers of the period, was inspired by dance forms of his time and created pieces of music based on the dances' tempi and rhythmic characteristics.

J.S. Bach

> Remember that the key of G minor has a Bb and an Eb in the key signature.

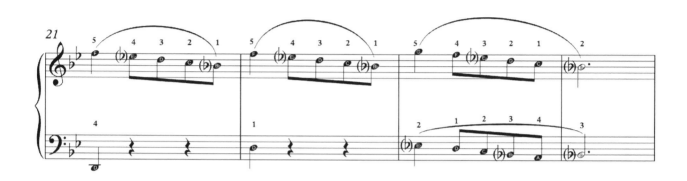

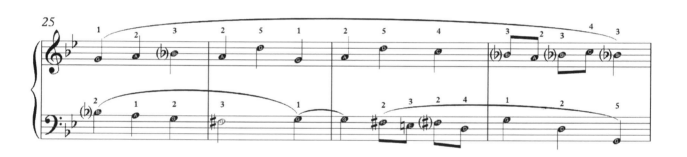

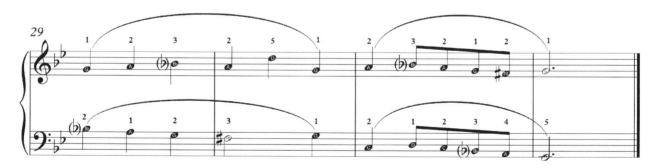

One last note: As you are learning these pieces, listen for the musical characteristics of the pieces in minor (like this one) and major (like the next one). There are no hard and fast rules about these characteristics of major and minor. However, exploring them might give you new musical insights.

Winter
(from the Four Seasons)

Antonio Vivaldi

Minuet in C Minor

J.S. Bach

Canon

The canon is a musical form that is similar to the song *Row, Row, Row Your Boat,* though more complicated in composition. This piece begins with one theme that is then repeated while other melodies and parts are added. The basic theme gradually grows and evolves, becoming more and more elaborate each return. This version employs arpeggios, running eighth notes, and chords in its various returns of the thematic material.

Johann Pachelbel

Adagio

For the first four measures, the right hand is one octave (eight notes) higher than written.

Go from the left hand to the right hand.

The left hand starts in the treble clef.

Move your third finger over.

Change to the bass clef.

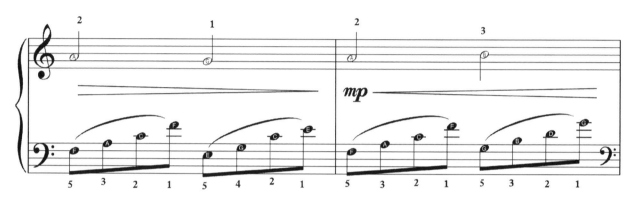

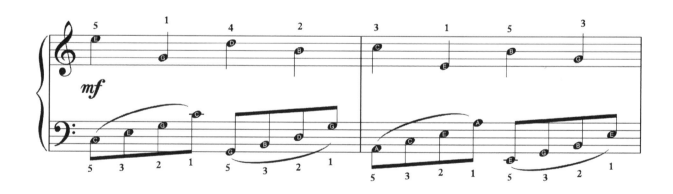

Lift your right hand and move to the next position.

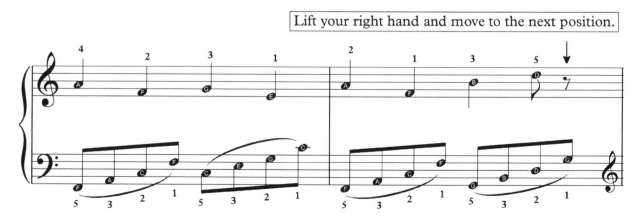

91

The right hand is one octave (eight notes) higher than written.

92

Pachelbel (1653-1706) was born in Nürnberg, Germany. He was a composer known for his organ works. He was one of the great organ masters of the generation before J.S. Bach.

Pachelbel's musical studies were at Altdorf and Regensburg. He held posts as an organist in Vienna and Studttgart. He also taught organ. One of his students was Johann Christoph Bach, who, in turn, gave his younger brother Johann Sebastian Bach his first formal keyboard lessons.

Pachelbel's Canon was relatively obscure until the late 20th century, when it experienced a surge in popularity. It was included in numerous television and movie soundtracks, most notably the film *Ordinary People* 1980). It has become a standard in general collections of classical music.

Minuet in G Major

Check Out Video 17

This is our third, and final, *Minuet in G Major.* Great job in getting this far in the book and learning so much outstanding music! You are building an impressive repertoire of pieces to play for family and friends.

J.S. Bach

Keep an ear and an eye out for the sequences that occur in measures 25, 26, and 27. Practice those three measures slowly, hands alone. Then, put both hands together and gradually increase the speed. Always look for musical patterns when learning a new piece.

Invention in C Major

Even though this piece is in C Major, there are a few sharps. Please keep an eye out for the F# notes that occur in the second half of the piece.

Once you learn the piece, try to build up the tempo (speed) of the music. Practice this little by little, always striving to be technically accurate.

J.S. Bach

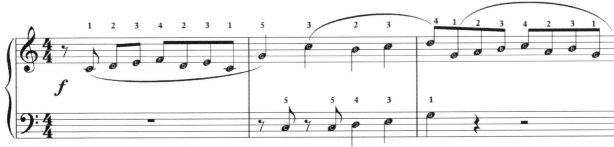

Count: 1 & 2 & 3 4

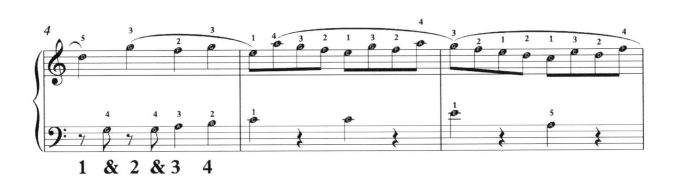

1 & 2 & 3 4

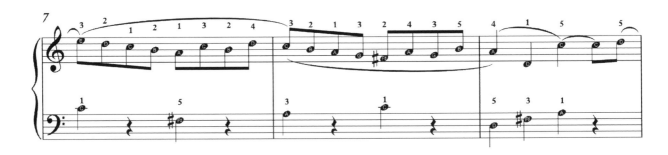

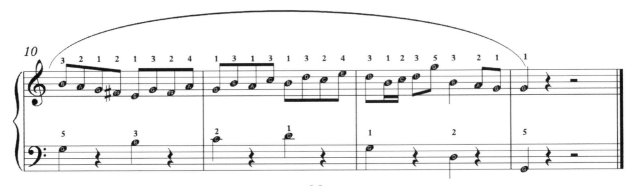

Bourrée

J.S. Bach

The right hand goes into the bass clef.

The right hand goes into the bass clef.

The right hand goes into the bass clef.

The right hand goes into the bass clef.

Aria

Domenico Scarlatti (1685-1757) is an Italian composer known for his 555 keyboard sonatas, which substantially expanded the technical and musical possibilities of the harpsichord. He was the son of the the composer Alessandro Scarlatti, who was famous for vocal music. Domenico Scarlatti was born in the same year as J.S. Bach and G.F. Handel.

Domenico Scarlatti

There are RH sequences in measures 4, 5, and 6.

Make the left-hand notes staccato (detached).

There are left-hand sequences in measures nine to twelve.

Make the left-hand notes legato (smooth) in contrast to the first left-hand section (measures one to eight).

Return to staccato playing in the left hand.

Practice these last four measures hands alone, first. Then add both hands.

98

Musette in D Major

Check Out Video 18

This is a lively, rhythmic piece of music. For much of the piece, the left hand will be your guide, in terms of keeping a steady beat. Take your time and learn one or two measures of the piece (hands alone) at a time. Then, put both hands together for one or two measures. Also, look and listen for patterns in the music. **Enjoy!**

J.S. Bach

This measure and measure 23 have syncopations: notes accented on weak parts of the beat. Keep a regular rhythm in your left hand, in order to play these syncopations easily. They should be played on the & of 2.

Remember to tie the D notes in measures 21 and 23.

Rigaudon

A Rigaudon (or Rigadoon) is a lively dance piece of the Baroque Period that is in 4/4 or 2/4 time signature. This particular Rigaudon features a technique called "imitation", which was very popular in the music of the period. In this case, the imitation occurs between the two hands; for example, in measure one and two (by the way, in music, we don't count partial measures), the left hand mimics what the right hand plays at the beginning. Something similar occurs between the hands in measures five and six.

Switch to treble clef in the left hand.

ff stands for fortissimo, which means "very loud".

101

Little Prelude in C Major

Here we have another wonderful piece by Bach. This music, like our previous piece, also uses the compositional technique of imitation between the two hands. While you are learning this piece, try to locate where the imitation occurs.

The piece also uses arpeggios (chords played one note at a time). Be prepared for a few finger stretches throughout the piece.

The phrases for the melody often start on the second eighth note of the measure.

J.S. Bach

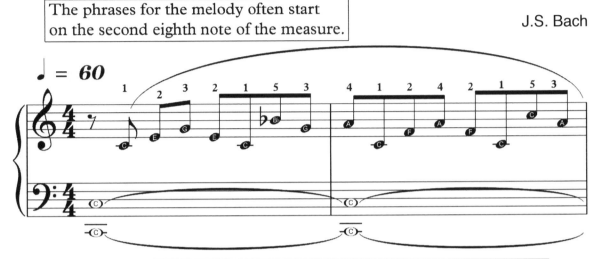

Hold these left-hand octaves for three measures: Twelves beats total.

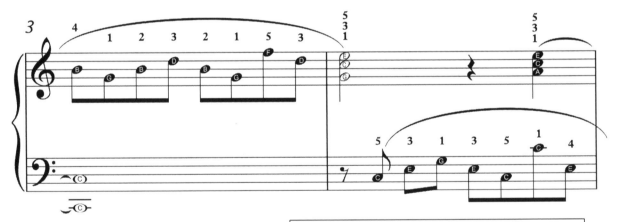

Practic these measures hands alone first.

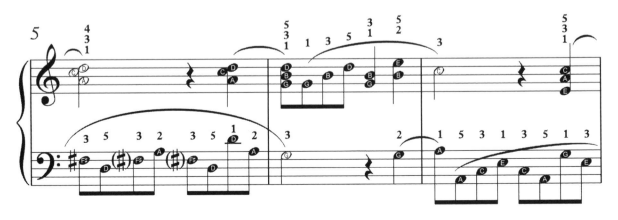

Invention
in A Minor

J.S. Bach

In these four measures, the left hand plays octaves: C to C, D to D, B to B, and C to C.

Play the first note of the measure with your left-hand thumb. Play the second note in these measures with the left-hand pinky (5th finger). Try to feel the distance between each octave. This is a very helpful piano skill to cultivate, since left-hand octaves occur in a great number of classical piano pieces. Try playing these four measures with left hand alone several times to get the feel for the hand stretch. Have fun!

The left hand plays in treble clef for this measure.

Hallelujah

George Frideric Handel

Invention in D Minor

J.S. Bach

Remember that there is a Bb in the key signature. We have marked the first few to help you.

Check Out Video 19

mf

These two measures imitate (copy) the musical idea from the first two measures, though playing the melody in a lower octave. Listen for other examples of imitation in the piece.

Play this right-hand trill quietly in order to bring out the melody in the left hand.

Play this left-hand trill quietly in order to bring out the melody in the right hand.

108

Check Out Video 20

Solfeggietto

C.P.E. Bach

The stems pointing up are for RH.
The stems pointing down are for LH.

Practice each system going into the first eighth note of the next system: 4 measure groups + one eighth note.

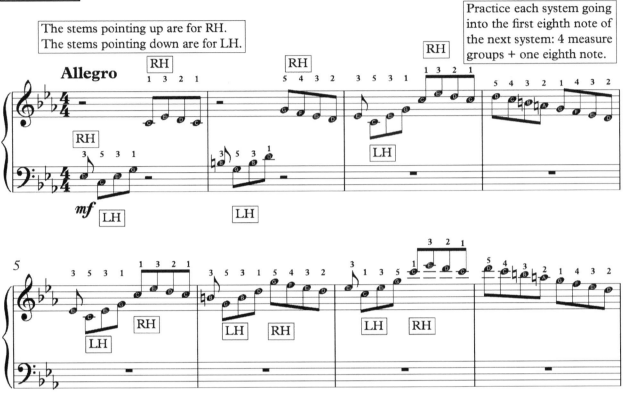

The left hand is played in the treble clef for this system.

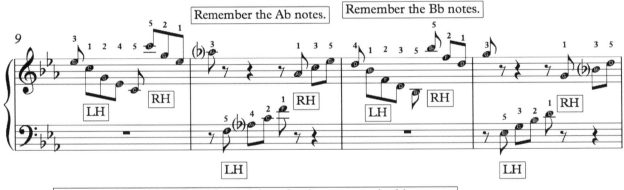

Remember the Ab notes.

Remember the Bb notes.

Alternate right and left hand for each beat for the measures in this system.

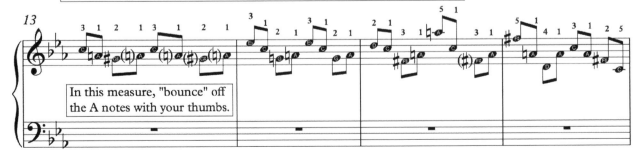

In this measure, "bounce" off the A notes with your thumbs.

The left hand is played in the treble clef for this system.

Remember the A-Natural and F-Sharp notes in these two systems.

Play the LH on the first and third downbeats; play the RH for the rest of the notes here. Follow the stem directions: Up for RH / Down for LH.

Remember the B-Flat notes in this measure.

Remember the B-Natural notes in this measure.

Remember the E-Flat notes in this measure.

Remember the E-Natural notes in this measure.

Play the LH on the first and third downbeats; play the RH for the rest of the notes here. Follow the stem directions: Up for RH / Down for LH.

Remember the E-Natural and A-Flat notes in these two systems.

Play the LH on the first and third downbeats; play the RH for the rest of the notes here. Follow the stem directions: Up for RH / Down for LH.

Think ahead in these first two measures and plan to land on the Db octaves with your left hand in measure three.

Second finger over the thumb here.

These notes are the same as the notes from two measures before, just an octave lower.

112

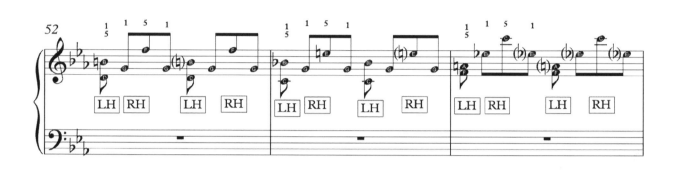

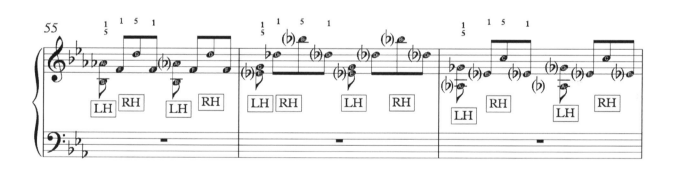

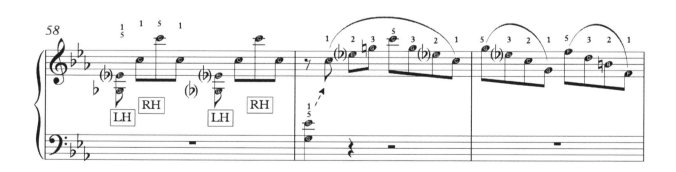

113

Bach Notes

Carl Philipp Emanuel Bach, the fifth child of J.S. Bach. He was a German, Classical Period musician and composer. His second name was given in honor of his godfather Georg Philipp Telemann, a friend of Johann Sebastian Bach. You may remember that we learned one of Telemann's pieces earlier on in this book.

C.P.E. Bach was one of the most important composers of the early Classical Period (the period that follows the Baroque Period in music history). C.P.E. Bach was his father's musical successor, in many ways. He felt that he never had any other teacher for composition and keyboard playing than his father, J.S. Bach.

C.P.E. Bach had a strong influence on the music of Haydn, Mozart, and Beethoven. The piece that we have learned in this book is a good example of C.P.E. Bach's precision of playing, beautiful touch, and intensity of emotion.

Congratulations!
You have completed the Book!

Great work in completing this book and video course on the music of J.S Bach for beginner piano. Along with expanding your repertoire of Baroque-period music, you now have an understanding of the fundamentals of piano playing: basic piano technique, beginner-level note reading and chord playing, and some understanding of music fundamentals--such as time signatures, beats, dynamics, staccato and legato notes, and the grand staff.

To continue to the next level, I would suggest two book and video courses:

1. *Beginner Classical Piano Music*
2. *Piano Scales, Chords & Arpeggio Lessons with Basic Music Theory*

Keep up the good work and continue to practice and play the piano!

Damon Ferrante

If you enjoyed this book, please recommend the paperback edition to your local library.

Damon Ferrante is a composer, guitarist, and professor of piano studies. He has taught on the music faculties of Seton Hall University and Montclair State University. For over 20 years, Damon has taught guitar, piano, composition, and music theory. Damon has had performances at Carnegie Hall, Symphony Space, and throughout the US and Europe. His main teachers have been David Rakowski at Columbia University, Stanley Wolfe at Juilliard, and Bruno Amato at the Peabody Conservatory of Johns Hopkins University. Damon has written two operas, a guitar concerto, song cycles, orchestral music, and numerous solo and chamber music works. He has over 30 music books and scores in print. For more information on his books, concerts, and music, please visit steeplechasearts.com.

More Best-Selling Music Books by Damon Ferrante!

Piano Scales Chords
Arpeggios Lessons

Book & Videos

Damon Ferrante

Beginner Classical Piano Music

Teach Yourself How to Play Famous Piano Pieces by Bach, Mozart, Beethoven & the Great Composers

Includes Streaming Videos!

Damon Ferrante

Book, Streaming Videos & MP3 Audio

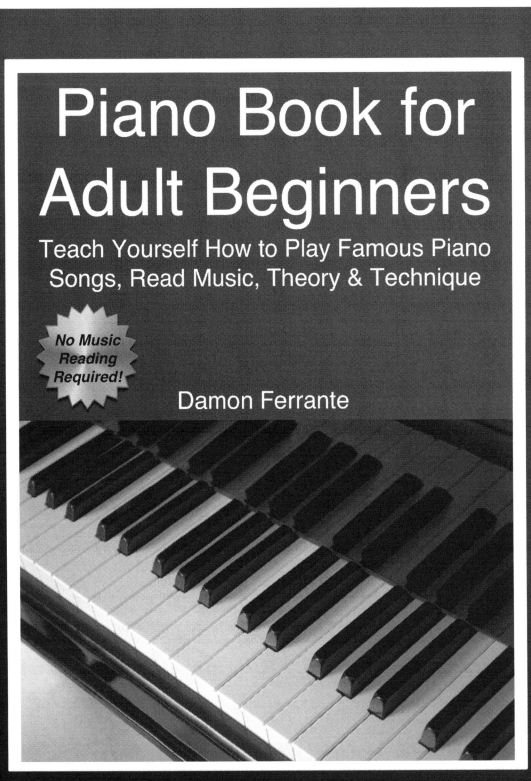

Piano Book for Adult Beginners

Teach Yourself How to Play Famous Piano Songs, Read Music, Theory & Technique

No Music Reading Required!

Damon Ferrante

Book & Streaming Video Lessons

Guitar Book for Adult Beginners

Teach Yourself How to Play Famous Guitar Songs, Guitar Chords, Theory & Technique

No Music Reading Required!

Damon Ferrante

Book & Streaming Video Lessons

Made in the
USA
Lexington, KY